CW00546606

A Starving People

BY THE SAME AUTHOR

The Diocese of Killaloe in the Eighteenth Century

The Diocese of Killaloe, 1800–1850

The Diocese of Killaloe, 1850–1904

AND A COMPANION TO THIS VOLUME

Before the Famine Struck: Life in West Clare, 1834–1845

A Starving People

Life and Death in West Clare, 1845–1851

Ignatius Murphy

IRISH ACADEMIC PRESS

Set in 10 on 12 point Bembo by
Verbatim Typesetting & Design, Dublin
and published by
IRISH ACADEMIC PRESS
Kill Lane, Blackrock, Co. Dublin, Ireland
and in North America by
IRISH ACADEMIC PRESS
c/o ISBS, 5804 NE Hassalo Street, Portland, OR 97213

© Estate of Monsignor Ignatius Murphy 1996

A catalogue record for this title
is available from the British Library.

ISBN 0-7165-2587-9

All rights reserved. No part of this publication may be re-
produced, stored or introduced into a retrieval system, or
transmitted, in any form or by any means (electronic,
mechanical, photocopying, recording or otherwise), without
the prior written permission of the copyright owner.

Printed in Ireland
by Colour Books Ltd, Dublin

Contents

To the memory of
the victims of the Famine in West Clare

Preface

This book and its companion, *Before the Famine Struck*, describe life in the parish of Kilfearagh in West Clare in the years before, during and after the Great Famine. Written almost thirty years ago for a Maynooth College degree, Fr Ignatius Murphy's study is now published for the first time.

No doubt the author, had he lived, would have reviewed his text in the light of Famine research in the intervening years. There is little need for revision, however, given the nature of the work and the competence of its author. I say this as a publisher, and latterly the author's publisher, having in 1990-95 published his massive three-volume history of the diocese of Killaloe in the eighteenth and nineteenth centuries. That history has been acclaimed as of national and not merely local significance, and certain to become a standard work.

For his case study, the author consulted manuscripts in Irish and British archives, parliamentary papers and other official documents of the period, contemporary newspapers and secondary sources. In order to throw into relief the full impact of the Famine, he did not confine himself to those terrible years alone. *Before the Famine Struck* (intended as a scene-setting introduction) provides a valuable account of life in a small Irish community before all changed.

The parish of Kilfearagh (see Map) covered 9,870 acres in the period under study. The land of the parish is poor and, though the bogs are an indication of ancient forests, few trees adorn the landscape (a tribute to the Atlantic breezes). A map made in 1811 marks the tiny village of 'Killqui', and in 1812 the first regular boat-service linked Kilrush and Limerick. By 1831 Kilkee had a population of about 1000 and was enjoying popularity as a holiday resort.

Over the parish as a whole, landlords and middlemen held sway. A 'strong farmer' was a tenant of 20-30 acres, with small farmers trying to survive on holdings of seven acres or less. Farming consisted mainly of tillage; and most of the grain was exported to England, leaving potatoes as the staple diet of the poor. Fish, harvested in currachs, was sold in Kilkee, Kilrush, Limerick and County Kerry. Turf was also produced in quantity.

Despite the rather grim social conditions, the lives of the people were by no means joyless. *Before the Famine Struck* describes old customs, the Kilkee Races, hurling and dancing on green and strand, the drink and temperance scenario, and faction fighting (as Kevin Danaher put it, 'nothing more than a crude and dangerous form of sport'); and then there were the visitors (includ-

ing day trippers) and a summer 'transplanting of a little Limerick' in the hotels
and lodges of Kilkee – all nicely and humorously described.

It was Mr Gay Murphy of Ennis, the author's brother, who proposed the
book for publication; he and his wife Randa were very helpful in the course
of its production; Eleanor Murphy read the proofs as did Brendan O'Cathaoir
(he had previously helped to prepare for publication the last volume of
Monsignor Murphy's *History*). The index was drafted by Brendan O'Cathaoir,
and the title for the second volume is his. Professor Vincent Comerford, St
Patrick's College, Maynooth, kindly provided a copy of the original text. The
Press is grateful for this support.

MICHAEL ADAMS

A People 'Half-Starved'

FAILURE OF THE POTATO CROP

During the summer of 1845 life went on very much as usual in Kilfearagh parish. There was quite a good number of visitors to the town of Kilkee, and in the countryside the prospects for a plentiful harvest were as good as in other parts of the country. And these prospects were bright indeed in the early part of the summer. In late May the *Limerick Chronicle* reported:

> Not a single failure has been reported in the potato crop ... Should it please Providence to continue the same favourable prosperity, the next harvest will be one of the earliest and most abundant remembered in this country.

Three months later the same newspaper was still very optimistic – the harvest would be a most abundant one. However, a week previously, a strange blight, which a few years earlier had made its appearance in North America, was detected in England, and such was the rapidity of its spread that it could only be a matter of time until Ireland also was affected. In early September the dread news came. On 13 September the English *Gardener's Chronicle* reported:

> We stop the Press with very great regret to announce that the potato Murrain has unequivocally declared itself in Ireland. The crops around Dublin are suddenly perishing ... where will Ireland be in the event of a universal potato rot?

Despite these warnings the *Clare Journal* was by no means alarmed. Having made an inquiry into the state of the crops, it announced on 18 September that an average crop was expected in Clare. But it did add that a complete picture could not be got until the time for digging the general crop at the end of October.

As the weeks slipped by in October it was becoming increasingly clear that there was a general failure of the potato crop and it was predicted that an early and prolonged famine would be the consequence unless immediate measures were taken at least to mitigate the calamity. In 1822 and 1830 the failures had been confined to areas in the west. In 1845 the damage to the potato crop was much more widespread. On 25 October the *Tipperary Vindicator* reported the prevalence of 'apprehensions of the most painful description'. And it continued:

We hope in the goodness of an all-wise Providence that He in his wisdom and bounty will spare this land from the tremendous scourge of famine and typhus, and open up the means of employment and sufficiency to a People who, in all their unheard of trials and sufferings, have ever steadfastly clung by the anchor of Faith.

Yet, even at this stage some continued to be optimistic. Mr John Fleming of Kilrush felt that the fears of many people were exaggerated. He had seen whole fields ruined by the blight. But he had also seen that many were only partially affected, while others again had emerged completely unscathed. In his opinion, if even half of the very abundant potato crop could be preserved there would be sufficient for all.

Mr Fleming's hopes were not to be realised. Even as he wrote his letter to the *Limerick Reporter* in early November it was only too clear that the people around him in West Clare were faced with starvation. The potatoes which had been pitted in sound condition were decaying, and already many families were suffering severe illness from eating diseased potatoes. Masses were offered up in the country chapels asking God to save the people from the almost inevitable disaster.

REMEDIAL MEASURES, AUTUMN–WINTER, 1845

Meanwhile the Government was growing increasingly alarmed by the reports being received about the potato crop, and in mid-October a commission was set up to suggest means of preserving potatoes which were sound when dug, of using diseased potatoes and of obtaining seed for the coming year. It surveyed the problem and issued suggestions, all of which proved valueless. At the end of October, unaware of the Government's inquiries and fearing that no preparations were being made, a committee of private citizens was formed at the Mansion House, Dublin, to examine the situation and propose remedies. And on 3 November a deputation including Daniel O'Connell, the Duke of Leinster and many other prominent citizens waited on the Lord Lieutenant to present him with their proposals. These called for the prohibition of food exports, the establishment of stores of food and relief machinery in each county and the provision of useful employment. The Lord Lieutenant, unaware of what the Government proposed to do, received them rather coolly and read a prepared non-committal statement.

A fortnight later the Government appointed a Relief Commission for Ireland and it held its first meeting on 20 November. Its immediate duty was to prepare to receive a supply of Indian corn meal which had already been ordered from the USA. And it also collected information from all parts of the country regarding the progress of the potato disease. Among its informants was Fr Michael Comyn, the PP of Kilfearagh and Killard, who gave such a gloomy description of the state of the crops in his parishes that the Commissioners immediately wrote to other people to find out if the situation was as described. The reply of Jonas Studdert (the Studderts were middlemen who leased part of the Conyngham lands: see below) showed that though he feared a scarcity he scarcely envisaged a famine. E.I. Morris, a coastguard who visited the area on the Commissioners' request, saw the dangers of the situation more clearly and noted the apprehensions of the people: 'I found the people everywhere quiet and civil, but under great alarm.' The dispensary doctor at Kilkee, John Griffin, on the other hand, was inclined to dismiss these fears and informed Assistant Commissioner John Hancock 'that every rational person in the parish was laughing at the statement made by certain parties relative to the state of the parish'.

In the meantime, following Fr Comyn's representations, the Commissioners had asked him for more information concerning his proposals regarding waste lands and fisheries. On 6 December, then, he forwarded a detailed petition on the second of these topics, promising a later one on waste lands. The development of deep sea fisheries he regarded as a positive way of countering the potato failure for many. In their present frail boats the fishermen could not venture out the twenty miles necessary to reach the rich fishing area. His reason for the poor fishing within twenty miles of the coast was a rather curious and ingenious one. He pointed out that originally the coast of Corca Baiscinn extended out for this distance, but an earthquake in the ninth century had submerged it. The former land area was still very little frequented by fish.

Shortly afterwards Fr Comyn visited the Commissioners in person to see what prospect of relief they held out to the poor in his parishes. After the meeting he felt that he had succeeded in convincing them that unless help was given within a short time the people would have no alternative to starvation. He also got a promise that they would impress on the Government the need for providing immediate employment in the area.

Fr Comyn was active, too, on another front at this time. At the weekly meeting of the Loyal National Repeal Association held at Conciliation Hall, Dublin, on 15 December, Mr John O'Connell remarked that a very interesting letter had been received from the Revd Mr Comyn, PP of Kilkee, with reference to the fisheries of Ireland and the great employment they could give to the people in the present state of distress. Fr Comyn certainly hoped to arouse more than mere interest on the part of John O'Connell and his father, the Liberator, who was also present. But when the letter had been read it was probably given no further thought. A few weeks before this the Mansion House Committee had been supplied with statistics concerning Kilfearagh and Killard parishes. In the townland of Kilfearagh it was pointed out to them, there were eighty-eight families whose total produce of potatoes was 1,450 barrels of which only 187 were good. At a meeting of the committee it was decided to bring these statistics to the attention of the government relief commission.

Back in West Clare the Kilrush Poor Law Guardians, among whom there were representatives from Kilfearagh parish, were also getting worried. At their meeting on 26 November, they drew up a petition to Queen Victoria asking her to call a meeting of Parliament as soon as possible in December to devise measures of averting the threatening famine. Another resolution very likely had the proposed Kilrush-Kilkee railway in mind:

> That it is suggested to have Parliament meet thus early to expedite the passing of Railway Bills and such other measures of employment as would enable the poor and working classes to purchase food and clothing during the approaching season of want and inclemency.

Less than four weeks later the chairman of the same Board of Guardians, Crofton Vandeleur made a personal contribution to the increase of misery when, a few days before Christmas, eight families were evicted from their little plots on his estate at Moyasta and their houses levelled before their eyes. This was a scene which was to be repeated many times in the ensuing years.

GOVERNMENT POLICY AND MEETINGS IN KILKEE

By the beginning of 1846 a four-point plan for combating the threat of famine had been devised by Sir Robert Peel and his Government:

1. The Relief Commissioners were told to form local committees composed of landowners, agents, magistrates, clergy and other residents of note. These committees would raise money locally out of which food could be bought for resale to distressed persons or even given free in urgent cases.
2. The Board of Works was to provide employment by making new roads – a procedure which had also been followed in previous famines.
3. Foreseeing that fever would inevitably follow destitution, it was directed that a separate fever hospital was to be got ready as soon as possible in connection with each workhouse.
4. As soon as food prices rose unreasonably some of the Indian corn in government stores was to be thrown on the market, to bring prices down.

To implement the first two points in this plan it was decided to call a meeting of gentlemen in each area where distress was expected. A representative of the Board of Works would attend and he would be able to ascertain what help local landlords were prepared to give, how many persons would need employment and what were the possibilities for works in the area. The first such meeting in the country was arranged for Kilkee on 10 January 1846, a choice probably suggested by Fr Comyn's earnest representations on behalf of his parishioners in the previous month and the evident hardship in the area.

From any point of view the Kilkee meeting could hardly be described as successful. The first difficulty arose when many people could not gain admittance to the meeting place owing to lack of space. The local magistrates were blamed for this as they had chosen the Billiard Room in preference to the more spacious National School which had been put at their disposal by Fr Comyn. At the meeting Henry Burton of Carrigaholt, the only resident landlord in the area, acted as chairman, with Robert FitzGerald of Donoughboy House, Kilkee, as vice-chairman and Dr Tuite of Kilkee as secretary. An official of the Board of Works, Mr Russell, was also present as was Mr C.W. Hamilton, agent for John MacDonnell, one of the two chief landlords in the parish (the other being Lord Conyngham).

The first resolution adopted indicated that although some potatoes were still available they were scarcely fit for human consumption:

> That the potatoes having now become so unfit for human use, that even the cattle are beginning to loathe them, the people are earnestly recommended to discontinue the use of any unless the few half-sound ones in hand, and that it becomes absolutely necessary for their sustenance to have immediate recourse to the consumption of bread at least once or twice a day, henceforward.

But how could the people make bread? Unaware that the Government was obtaining Indian corn, the meeting called for the opening of storehouses at Doonbeg and Kilkee – for the purchase and preservation of the remnant of corn still left in the country. Another resolution called for the immediate passing of the Kilrush-Kilkee Railway Bill and the gathering also endorsed *in toto* a memorial adopted at a New Year's Day meeting in Kilkee. This earlier meeting had made a number of suggestions for providing employment in the area. These included the provision of harbour facilities in Doonbeg Bay; the building of some coast roads leading from Kilkee – to Baltard Tower on one side and to Dunlickey Castle and Reahy Hill on the other; a few embankments against the tide on Kilkee beach and the building of a landing slip for Kilkee fishermen. Finally, the proceedings on 10 January ended with the appointment of a local committee.

The meeting in the Billiard Room had been held in the morning. Then, in the afternoon, a number of people with landed interests locally, some of whom had been present at the earlier meeting, met at the West End Hotel, and drew up a rival memorial for presentation to the Government. What was the reason for this second gathering? Jonas Studdert, in a letter to Sir Lucius O'Brien, gave the landowners' viewpoint:

As I apprehended, our meeting of yesterday was interrupted by Mr Comyn, assisted by Mr Robert FitzGerald, Doctor Tuite, and at the head of a large mob. Everything was carried by shouting from the people tutored by him. No committee formed, but at the latter part of the day he proposed a Committee not having the slightest regard for the mode of choosing one as directed by you. And in fact mostly composed of his own relations ... Mr Russell was treated as a menial under their orders and not even allowed to explain what his instructions were ...

Mr C.W. Hamilton commented that it was only with great difficulty that Fr Comyn had succeeded in getting Mr Burton into the chair, but then stood by him and proposed his resolutions himself without reference to the chair. However, Mr Hamilton pointed out that the letter convoking the meeting had specified that all interested parties were invited. Therefore Fr Comyn 'had naturally grounds for making it a mob meeting'.

The rival meetings and the resolutions adopted at them meant that nobody was satisfied with the day's happenings. Those who took part in the second meeting were clearly dissatisfied with what had taken place at the first – while many of the local people were quite indignant with those of the gentry who participated in the second gathering. And this indignation was strongly expressed in a resolution adopted at a meeting held in Kilkee Catholic Chapel on 18 January:

> That we scout with indignation the pigmy efforts of certain gentlemen and others, who, without license [*sic*] or authority from the people or government, formed themselves into a self-constituted Board at a meeting stealthily got up after the regular proceedings of the day.

All this was not a very promising start to the hoped-for joint local effort to combat the distress, and although on the surface harmony was soon achieved, the undercurrents of tension remained, breaking out every now and again. On 16 March 1847, Captain Mann, a local Coastguard officer, wrote to Charles Trevelyan, Assistant Secretary to the Treasury and in overall charge of Irish famine relief:

> Grieved am I to say that in other cases party and jealous feeling produces most baneful consequences; a sad proof came before me a few days since as regards that wretched place Kilkee, where I fear dissension will never cease to do mischief, and the poor to suffer by it, instead of their being united in exertion to do good, casting aside all selfish and other feelings; there it is the very reverse, and how to cure this it is impossible to say.

To the Government, too, the Kilkee meetings proved a big disappointment. It had been hoped that the meeting arranged there would set a
precedent for other such gatherings, but Sir Randolph Routh, chairman of
the Relief Commission, was of the opinion that instructions to be issued
would now have to be re-modelled in the light of the Kilkee experience.
The chief cause of disappointment was the lack of any offers of local contributions. These had not even been mentioned at the first meeting, while at
the second the gentry had merely made a vague reference to the repayment
by instalment of loans for public works. Jonas Studdert wrote in this connection: 'It is clear money will not be placed at the disposal of such mad specula-
tors,' referring to Fr Comyn and his supporters. One feels that this was an
excuse rather than a reason for non-contribution, for a few days later Mr
C.W. Hamilton informed the Relief Commissioners in Dublin that under
the present difficulties the proprietors would not be able to make any contributions nor could they offer sufficient security for the future repayment of
loans.

Yet, despite this disappointment, in a letter to Trevelyan, Routh did
admit that the distress in the Kilkee area was undeniable, and he pointed out
that it was for the Government to decide, in the light of all the facts, how
much employment they would be prepared to give at the public expense to
meet the immediate want.

KILKEE RELIEF COMMITTEE

Despite the squabbles a local relief committee soon got down to work and
appointed Fr Comyn and the Revd James Martin, the Church of Ireland
rector, to conduct an investigation into the condition of the people in the
neighbourhood. The result of their work was put to the members at a
meeting in late February at which Mr Russell of the Board of Works was also
present. The report stated very emphatically that 160 householders and their
families were in a state of abject poverty and nearly deprived of every earthly
means of subsistence. Some potatoes were still available but pigs and fowl
which had been fed on them for the previous two months were now found to
have diseased livers. 'The stench of these potatoes when boiled is so offensive
and unbearable, that the people rush out of the cabin with the iron pot in
their hands, lest the effluvium should cause a fever, and they let them remain
some time outside, in order that the fresh air may pass through them, for
others, even those who are starving, are unable to touch them.' Even when
the best parts had been picked out they were still very unpalatable. Many
people had been eating these since November, and it seemed impossible that
they should be able to escape disease as a consequence. In the final analysis
then:

The actual fact is that hundreds of people here, are, what would be understood in England as 'starved' and what is understood in Ireland as 'half-starved'. Their cheeks are hollow and transparent, the mouth enlarged, the nose pinched in, the eyes glassy or else of a watery clearness. They scarcely utter any complaints; they do not beg of anyone walking about the village, but follow him silently in a crowd.

This analysis was borne out by an official report made about the same time by Dr John Griffin. He pointed out that a form of fever had been prevalent in the locality for the previous three or four months, and this was to be attributed, in some degree at least, to the use of unsound potatoes. Unless protective measures were taken to avert the threatened famine, an outbreak of disease could also be expected. And on 22 February he told the Relief Commissioners that a fever hospital in the area would be of very great help in checking the spread of fever. All this was in marked contrast to his attitude in the previous December when interviewed by Mr Hancock.

It was against this background that the Kilkee Relief Committee outlined to the Lords of the Treasury in mid-March the plight of the people in the area, pointing out that the Board of Works engineer was awaiting Treasury sanction to start relief works which would give much needed employment. To demonstrate the seriousness of the situation they remarked that the people were now beginning to eat the potatoes which had been kept for seed – a point which was also made in a memorial from the inhabitants of the townland of Kildimo to the Lord Lieutenant. The final conclusion of the Kilkee Relief Committee was that the corn purchased by the Government should be immediately distributed in the area. And a week later a somewhat similar plea was made by Colonel Vandeleur. To offset the high prices being demanded for provisions, the Government should send its Indian corn to Kilrush and Kilkee and sell it to the poor who had obtained tickets authorising them to receive it – a suggestion which was in line with the Government's policy for the control of food prices. At this period, according to Captain Mann, who had been put in charge of relief at Kilrush, the portion of Kilrush Workhouse allotted to Kilfearagh district was nearly full.

Meanwhile Sir Randolph Routh was complaining that the landed gentry in the Kilrush-Kilkee area seemed to be determined to make no financial contributions towards providing relief. However, on 31 March he was able to tell Trevelyan that Colonel Vandeleur had given £50 – a beginning at least had been made. But in Kilkee there were no unsolicited contributions and the Relief Committee was showing no signs of requesting any. Finally, in early May, under threat of refusal of meal supplies by Captain Mann, it appealed for funds and circularised people with landed interests and wealthy lodge-owners who were living outside the parish. By 12 May only one of the absentees, John MacDonnell, had responded with a contribution (£8), although it would appear that soon afterwards Lord Conyngham gave £10. The Revd James Martin remarked that the local farmers would willingly contribute but were unable. However, Jonas Studdert gave £8, Fr Comyn £5 and the Revd James Martin £5. In all £38.2s. 0d. had been gathered by 12 May. To this, on the advice of Poor Law commissioner Sir Edward Twisleton, the Lord Lieutenant added £23. It was stated that the money would be used to provide food for those in extreme want and give employment to women and children during the summer season. The secretary of the committee (Hugh Hogan, a Kilkee businessman) also pointed out, with an eye to the holiday season, that arrangements would be made to prevent strolling beggars from annoying the visitors.

In March the Relief Committee took steps in another direction also. It was decided that an industry could do a good deal for the town and parish, and Hugh Hogan, as secretary of the committee, was instructed to enter into communication with Messrs Wallace, Sharpe and Co., of Glasgow with a view to starting the manufacture of lace and muslin in Kilkee. Mr Hogan wrote to the firm concerned giving details of the population, etc., of the area. The reply did offer some hope that in the not too distant future the firm might extend its activities to Kilkee – but no further moves seem to have been made in the matter.

EFFORTS OF FR COMYN AND HUGH HOGAN

Fr Comyn and Hugh Hogan were both members of the Relief Committee, but they were also very active as private individuals in trying to do something for the people. In mid-January Fr Comyn again wrote to the Relief Commission in Dublin and, in his promised petition on the subject, tried to press home his views on the development of the wastelands in his parishes. 'It is evidently better,' he wrote, 'to locate our surplus population on these unprofitable wastes in their own native land, than compel them to emigrate to some foreign and hostile disposed country to Great Britain, to swell the ranks of her enemies; or be obliged to maintain them in idleness at home in workhouses, at the public expense.' Such development, however, could only come about if the wastelands were taken by compulsion from the landlords who were neglecting to do anything about them. Fr Comyn also lacerated John MacDonnell for his failure to give any encouragement to the development of potter's clay which lay in his land within a mile of Kilkee. Two months later, on 22 March, at a meeting in Kilkee Repeal Reading Room a memorial was drawn up for the local application of the provisions of a recent drainage act.

Fr Comyn also brought the troubles of his parish to the notice of William

Smith O'Brien. At a conference of Irish MPs held in Dublin towards the end of January O'Brien alluded to a conversation he had with Fr Comyn, a few days previously, in which Fr Comyn told him that the condition of the poor in his neighbourhood was most deplorable.

At first sight the fishermen might seem to be far better off than those who were depending exclusively on the produce of the soil. Even when the potatoes failed (for each had his little plot of ground) they could still turn to the sea. But the winter of 1845-6 proved to be a particularly disappointing one for fishing, so that when spring came the fishermen were, if anything, even worse off than their neighbours. In late January, following up the idea proposed by Fr Comyn to the Relief Commissioners in December, Hugh Hogan wrote to Mr Robert Greene of the Irish Deep Sea Fishing Company, regarding the prospects for fishing in West Clare and received a very encour-agng reply. Mr Greeen promised to purchase all fish caught, but he pointed out that little could be done without facilities. However, he felt confident that any petition to the Government would get a favourable hearing.

Hugh Hogan, having thus ensured a market for any fish caught, now began to gather information for a petition. He discovered that the local fisher-men were in such dire straits that not only had some of them pawned or sold their beds or clothes but many had even pawned their fishing nets in Kilrush. Immediately he wrote to Mr Jeremiah Dowling, the pawnbroker, requesting details. The reply was revealing. Mr Dowling had seventy-two nets from the Kilkee area in pawn, on which he had paid out £15. But this was not all. He went on to write: 'So great is the distress among the fishermen that I think if they could convey their boats to the office we would have them also.'

The first memorial drawn up by Hogan was to the Lord Lieutenant, asking for a grant or loan to supply the necessary requisites for deep-sea fishing. The reply was unfavourable, and Mr Hogan tried again – this time in a petition to Parliament which was presented to the House of Commons on 9 March. Again he met with no success, although a few days previously a bill which was very relevant to his petition received the royal assent. This was an act which provided an annual sum of money, £5,000, for the construction of piers and harbours. As a last resort Mr Hogan wrote to the Prime Minister himself, Sir Robert Peel, with similar negative results.

Meanwhile, during the month of March, Mr Greene had sent a representa-tive, Mr Fraser, to Kilkee to report on the possibilities for development in the area. And while in West Clare, Mr Fraser, at the direction of his employ-er, secured the release from pawn of all the nets of the Kilkee fishermen. It was probably as a result of this visit that Mr Greene decided to establish an agency in Kilkee for the curing and preserving of fish. He also promised to open a loan-office to help and encourage needy fishermen. We have no evi-dence, however, as to whether these promises ever came to fruition. If the condition of the fishermen had not been improved, this was certainly no fault of Hugh Hogan's, and, as a token of their gratitude for his efforts on their behalf, they volunteered their services and cut his turf in early May.

PUBLIC WORKS

Whatever private individuals or the local Relief Committee did, the fate of the people of Kilfearagh parish depended on the manner of implementation of government policy in the area. As remarked later by Captain Mann, this involved the taking of three steps:

1. The poor had to be provided with the means of earning money wages.
2. A substitute food for the potato had to be introduced.
3. Owing to the absence of small shopkeepers who would deal in Indian meal, those operating the relief scheme would have to take their place and sell it in small quantities here and there throughout the peninsula.

The first of these steps was seen to by the Board of Works' public relief schemes. In early February the magistrates and cesspayers of Moyarta barony met and petitioned for the commencement of certain specified works. But as the meeting was got up with great haste, the actual descriptions of the proposed works and the estimated costs were not sufficiently accurate for immediate implementation. Mr Russell, the Board of Works engineer, on this account, felt that it would take some time to get the works underway, as more exact calculations would have to be made. However, he thought that a beginning could be made with some hill-cutting and improvements. A week later, on 25 February, the Commissioners of Public Works recommended a number of projects in Moyarta barony to the Treasury, including the following in Kilfearagh parish:

£300 for the improvement of the Kilkee-Kilrush Road.
£900 for a road from Kilkee along the cliffs to the mills at Moveen.
£30 for the improvement of the Corbally-Lislanihan Road.
£60 for cutting the hills on the Corbally Road.
£100 for the Kildimo-Emlagh Road.

For these works, if finally approved, the Government would advance the full cost, of which half would be in the form of a loan to be repaid by the local landowners over a period of years.

In the meantime Mr Russell had returned to Kilkee with employment tickets. Employment on the projected public works would generally be given only to a holder of one of these tickets, which were to be distributed at meetings of the local Relief Committee to those who were considered unable to provide food for their families. In Kilkee, as final approval from the Treasury for the projects was awaited, people applied for these tickets – but, at first, not nearly as many did so as had been expected. In their report on the district in late February, Fr Comyn and the Revd Mr Martin tried to give an explanation for this. The country people, in their opinion, were under the impression that the townspeople would get first preference and therefore did not apply for employment in such numbers as their extreme want would warrant. In all there were only forty applications from the country and 160 from the town. However, at this stage it looked as if only fifty of these would get immediate employment – at 10*d*. a day.

By early March, when work had not yet begun, people began to grow impatient – and in their memorial to the Treasury of about 7 March the Kilkee Relief Committee reminded the Treasury officials that their sanction was being awaited. A few days later 250 men were given employment, but this only whetted the appetite for more work. On 19 March a letter-writer in the *Clare Journal* complained that in Kilkee scarcely one man in twenty was employed, notwithstanding the extraordinary exertions of its inhabitants and clergy.

The main projects being undertaken were the building of a new road from the West End to Look Out Cliff and thence to Dunlickey Castle and beyond; and the building and levelling of the hills on the Kilrush-Kilkee Road. It was hoped that, by means of the latter project, passenger cars would be enabled to make the journey from Kilkee to Kilrush in an hour instead of an hour and a half. The embankment of the cliff on the west side of Kilkee, which had long been in a dangerous condition, was also begun.

Other possibilities for works were also being proposed, and agreement was reached that a coast road between Kilkee and Doonbeg by Chimney Bay and Baltard Castle was desirable. And in March the tenants on Lord Conyngham's estate sent a memorial to their landlord asking him to contribute, along with the Board of Works, towards making a carriageway or embankment round the bay. In late April a promise of a contribution of £100 was received – if the Board of Works undertook the project.

After work on the various schemes had begun, the number of employed rose rapidly. On 28 March the Board of Works had 1,600 employed in Clare. Three days later the figure was 5,487 and on 7 April it had risen to 10,870. In Kilkee and Doonbeg parishes 620 were employed in mid-May and further applications were being received.

The rate of payment on the public works for men was, we have seen, 10*d*. a day. Strong boys got 8*d*. and small boys received 6*d*. These wages were supposed to be under the general current rate in order to encourage people to take up other employment if available. In a letter to the Relief Commissioners at the end of January, Mr. C.W. Hamilton protested at this arrangement. If a man did not get sufficient wages he would have to enter the Poorhouse in order to feed his family and, in Hamilton's view, this would be disastrous as it would strike at the independence of the labourer's character.

There could be other difficulties, too, in the practical day-to-day administration of the works. On 9 June 1846, the Revd James Martin wrote to the Relief Commissioners complaining of the undue amount of power exercised rather arbitrarily by some of the gangers. 'If it suits their convenience they will take a recommendation from the committee – if it does not – they will reject it.' And he enclosed a petition from one poor labourer who felt he had been victimised. This is of sufficient interest to reproduce in full:

TO THE SITTING COMMITTEE OF PUBLIC WORKS OF KILKEE

The Humble Petition of James Carrig of Kilfiera most humbly showeth

That your petr. having Five in family to support and not a morsel of food since Christmas last but what he earned by his daily labour, petr. got into the public works when the Cliff Road commenced, and continued until last Saturday fortnight, he petr. gave one day's work to a man that gave him a basket of black potatoes for his little children to pick, and came to work on the Monday following as usual. When about 12 o'clock on said day Sullivan the Steward dismissed him and would not allow him even that half days wages.

    Then when petr. was murmuring for having him dismissed Sullivan desired him go to the Priest and that if he gave him a ticket he would take him in the work which petr. did obtain from the Priest, and got but one days work afterwards. Your petr having pawned his coat for which he only got 2s. to buy provisions for his family. And that himself and them are living these three days back on one meal a day Your petr is surprised that any Committee would allow this imposter Sullivan to go on in this manner when they have a power to discontinue such infernal practice
Your petr will pray
James Carrig

On the receipt of the Revd Mr Martin's complaint, the Relief Commissioners decided to make an inquiry into the matter and get further information from the Board of Works.

INDIAN MEAL

With the provision of employment the first step had been taken, as some money was now in circulation. The next necessity was to provide an alternative to the potato, which, as we have seen [in *Before the Famine Struck*], was the staple diet of the average smallholder and labourer. In areas like West Clare cooking any other food had become a lost art. As Trevelyan wrote: 'There is scarcely a woman of the peasant class in the west of Ireland whose culinary art exceeds the boiling of a potato. Bread is scarcely ever seen and an oven is unknown.' But when there were no potatoes, what was to be done? In late 1845 the Government realised that famine was threatening and it obtained supplies of Indian corn from America – not to replace the potato or feed the people but to be kept in reserve and released on the market when provision prices rose unduly. In fact, however, in the early summer of 1846 this Indian meal was to stand between many people and utter starvation.

When supplies of the corn arrived in Ireland in early 1846, depots were established throughout the country in various centres including Kilrush. In March, Captain Mann began to issue it at a cheap rate in Kilrush, but as yet the distribution seems to have been confined to this central depot. During May minor depots were set up at various points in West Clare including one at the Coastguard Boathouse, Kilkee – all exactly as Colonel Vandeleur had petitioned some time previously.

The provision of Indian meal did not, however, solve all problems, for, at first, it seemed quite likely that people would not eat it. Previous experience had prejudiced them against it, and in some areas it become known as 'Peel's brimstone'. Captain Mann soon found that the reaction in West Clare was anything but favourable as the people feared unpleasant effects. However, Fr Kenny, PP of Kilrush, decided that this prejudice would have to be combated in a practical manner and for two weeks 'all but lived entirely with two curates, on the meal made into bread and stirrabout'.

As a result of Fr Kenny's example the problem soon was not one of disposal but of ensuring a sufficient supply of meal. The corn was received unground and so had to be brought to a mill before sale. In Kilrush, while Mr Paterson's mill had a plentiful supply of water and remained working, all was well, but there was at least one occasion when it was out of action for three days. And when it did break down, there was nobody at hand who had an expert knowledge of its workings.

The problem experienced in Kilrush in May was one which had to be faced elsewhere also – the uncertainty or inadequacy of facilities for grinding. In Kilkee a man who was occasionally employed as a coastguard brought up one answer. He began manufacturing querns which he sold for 10s. and 12s. Others followed his example, and by early November 1846 quite a nice little trade had been established. However, one is inclined to have some reservations about the grinding qualities of these querns. When interviewed by Captain Mann, the originator of the project said that he had already ground horse-beans and by a little manipulation he felt sure he would also be able to grind Indian corn.

Just at this time Trevelyan was toying with the idea that, as there were not sufficient mills, the people should grind the corn themselves. He had been searching for specimens which could be copied, and at first succeeded only in getting an 'inferior Indian model'. Later, he managed to get a better specimen from the Shetland Islands. When word came, then, of what was happening in Kilkee, Trevelyan was very interested and anxious to see one of the querns. He wrote personally to Captain Mann who immediately went to Kilkee and bought one of them to send to Routh as Trevelyan had requested.

A month later Mann wrote to Routh: 'The value of our common quern is now fully proved. Scarcely a cabin but has one and a great many are being taken away to other parts. The farmers and peasantry generally are grinding their own grain.' And in the beginning of January 1848, Twisleton told Trevelyan that the handmills had been distributed to the different unions throughout the country: 'I have not heard anything about the effect of them. Still they were a useful present, and I feel obliged to you for them.'

When discussing the importation of the Indian corn, an obvious question to be asked is – Why Indian corn at all? What happened to the corn and other food produced locally? Perhaps the best answer to this question is contained in a letter written by Routh to Trevelyan on 1 January 1846. Routh pointed out that the Irish people did not regard wheat, oats and barley as food – these were grown to pay the rent, and to pay the rent was the first necessity of life in Ireland. It would be a desperate man who ate up his rent, with the certainty before him of eviction and death by slow torture. And this is exactly what happened in Kilfearagh parish in 1846. Even though the people had corn and other produce, these had to be sold to pay the rent. As a result, when the situation was rather desperate in early March before relief employment had begun, Kilrush port was busy exporting. According to Captain Mann: 'We were literally stopped by carts laden with grain, butter, bacon etc., being taken to the vessels loading from the quay. It was a strange anomaly, and well might be said, could not be matched but in this country.' And in the final week of April the *Clare Journal* reported that 3,500 quarters of grain had been exported from Kilrush to London and Glasgow. Yet, despite this anomalous situation the people survived, mainly because of the Indian meal, and looked forward with hope and fear to the next harvest.

A Second Failure

As 1845 gave way to 1846 some people were already thinking of the coming harvest and the possibility of avoiding a recurrence of the disease. At a public meeting held in Kilkee on New Year's Day, 1846, this subject was discussed, and in a memorial drawn up for the Relief Commissioners it was claimed that reclaimed bogland alone could be confidently expected to produce sound potatoes in the coming autumn. The memorial states:

> Your memorialists beg to assure you that their apprehensions are very considerable, and that they feel loth to venture tilling the land heretofore growing potatoes, fearing that it retains the Malaria that has been so fatal the last season. We also fear that the contagion has been wafted by the wind to the neighbouring cornfields so that we look with confidence to the BOGLANDS ALONE for a secure supply of potatoes for after seasons.
>
> This is not the conclusion your memorialists alone have arrived to, but is the opinion also of skilful and scientific men.

Mr G.H. FitzGerald of Kilkee concerned himself with another aspect of the problem – sufficiency of seed potatoes. In a letter to the *Limerick Chronicle* in March he claimed that after having made several experiments with diseased potatoes he had discovered a process which destroyed all infectious matter and made them safe and clean for seed. His process was a simple one – steeping the potatoes for a few minutes in a solution of bluestone. At the same time he also sent a letter to the chairman of the Relief Committee in Dublin informing him of his discovery. Although quite confident of his success in March, no doubt he found reason to revise his views when autumn came again.

As the days of summer passed by, all eyes were on the new crop of potatoes. The Government was determined to keep fully informed of developments, and, long before the crisis time had arrived, sent for reports on the situation from constables throughout the country. Reporting for Kilfearagh parish on 29 May, Constable Robert Griffin stated that a quarter of the arable land had been planted with potatoes, a decrease from the previous years when about one-third had been similarly used. Of this, somewhat less than one-third had been let in conacre. A notable feature, perhaps inspired by the theories advanced at the meeting on New Year's Day, 1846, was that more bog had been tilled than for years previously – despite a decrease in the overall acreage.

On 21 July, as harvest-time approached, a Treasury minute directed that all relief schemes be stopped, except in certain unusual cases. However, on various excuses most continued to function but not, it would seem, in Kilfearagh. Towards the end of July the local Relief Committee made a plea for three or four weeks' further employment. Otherwise 'we apprehend that riots may be the consequence.' On the very day of writing a crowd had assembled and threatened to break open the meal stores if they were not given the means of subsistence. And about the same time Jonas Studdert reported that want of money had already induced many to plunder the potato fields.

But what of the potato fields? On 31 July and 1 August, Mr T. Smith made an inspection in Kilfearagh parish and, in general, found the potato crop in a fairly healthy condition. However, in Lisdeen he detected three acres of diseased potatoes and in Farrihy two more. These were signs of what was to come – and the change came so suddenly that it was scarcely possible to believe it. In the words of Captain Mann, reporting from the western peninsula of Clare:

> I shall never forget the change in one week in August. On the first occasion, on an official visit of inspection, I had passed over thirty-two miles thickly studded with potato fields in full bloom. The next time the face of the whole country was changed, the stalk remained bright green but the leaves were all scorched black. It was the work of a night, distress and fear was pictured on every countenance, and there was a general rush to dig and sell, or consume the crop by feeding pigs or cattle, fearing in a short time they would prove unfit for any use. Consequently there was a very wasteful expenditure, and distress showed itself much earlier than in the preceding season.

The disaster was total. As the potatoes were generally set in mid-May, their growth was therefore checked in less than three months. What was left was no bigger than a marble, completely black, not a quarter ripe and hastening to decomposition when taken out of the ground. In 1845 the failure had been partial and, at the very worst, the people had half-sound potatoes to eat for a long period. In 1846 the blight had come earlier and had spared nothing. As early as 11 August an official reporting on Galway and Clare was able to say:

> I am therefore clearly of the opinion that the scarcity of the potato last year will be nothing compared with this, and that, too, several months earlier.

NEW GOVERNMENT PLANS FOR RELIEF

On 9 August a correspondent from Kilkee writing to the editor of the *Tipperary Vindicator* called on the Government to come forward and save the people from inevitable ruin. The Mansion House Committee should be reconvened, while the corn should not be allowed out of the country as in the previous year. Eight days later Lord John Russell, the new premier, informed the Commons that 'the prospect of the potato crop is even more distressing than last year,' and that extraordinary measures for relief should be taken. The measures adopted were, in fact, anything but extraordinary and were scarcely calculated to satisfy the writer from Kilkee.

1. Public works would again be undertaken but, unlike the previous year when the British Government bore half the cost, all the cost would now have to be met by the district where the works would be carried out. Presentment sessions, or meetings of ratepayers to discuss the works to be undertaken in a district, would be held as before, but instead of being voluntary they would now have to be summoned by the Lord Lieutenant. Works proposed had to get the approval of and would then be carried out by the Board of Works. The Treasury would advance the cost, but it would have to be repaid within ten years by means of a rate levied on all poor-rate payers in the locality, that is, those possessed of some means. In addition, the Government allocated £50,000 for grants to districts too poor to bear the whole cost of public works. Finally, all relief schemes undertaken were to last no longer than a year and to be wound up by 15 August 1847.

2. With a slight exception the Government would neither import nor supply any food. As Captain Mann wrote: 'The object of the second series commencing September, 1846, was to endeavour to turn the supply of food to the country into its legitimate channel, the Trade.' And Trevelyan pointed out that merchants could not be expected to get in big stocks if there was a possibility of their being undersold by the Government. However, west of the Shannon and in a few other areas, government food depots would be established here and there – but these were to be opened only as a last resort when private traders had failed to provide supplies of food.

3. Members of local Relief Committees were no longer to be elected but nominated by the Lieutenant of the country – which, of course, meant the disbanding of existing committees. The new committees would not be able to issue employment tickets – they would only be allowed to provide lists of persons eligible for employment. Subscriptions would still be collected locally for relief, but the government contribution would not exceed one half at most.

WAITING FOR RELIEF WORKS TO BEGIN

About the same time as the blight struck again, the meal depots closed their doors. The new relief plans had not yet come into operation, so that the people were thrown back on their own resources, which were practically non-existent. The cessation of the relief works meant that many had neither food nor the means of obtaining it. On 27 August Fr Malachy Duggan wrote:

> The suspension of Public Works here and the sale of Indian Meal almost contemporaneous, has excited a degree of alarm among the people, not easily conceived, and will probably be as fatal in its consequences as any measure the Government could adopt under existing circumstances

And four days previously, on Sunday 23 August, a petition for presentation to the Government, outlining the position in the parishes, had been signed by over 4,000 people at the chapels of Kilkee and Doonbeg. The picture painted was not a very pleasant one:

> Up to the first of this present month your petitioners have been cheered by the prospect of an abundant harvest, the potato gardens looked so luxuriant, but at present, through all parts of this extensive district, nothing meets the eye but withered leaves and stalks, emitting a most intolerable odour, and the esculents that ought to be fit for use are perfectly black, almost unfit for feeding swine. They look for employment, some relief and a reconsideration of the Poor Law valuation in the parish, with a view to exempting the poorer classes of occupiers from taxation.

And the petition ended as follows:

> N.B. Diarrhoea and other diseases are already rife in this district, doing the work of death slowly, yet surely.

An official reply was soon received, which promised that if an inquiry were held and the statements in the petitions were found to be correct, the Lord Lieutenant would lose no time in putting into operation the acts through which relief might be afforded to the people. Immediately Fr Comyn appointed men who visited every townland in the parish and estimated the provisions available to each individual family. It was found that in the whole parish of Kilkee there was not sufficient corn, meal, flour and potatoes to last, upon an average, for one month. The returns were then checked and confirmed by the Relief Committee, after which Fr Comyn set out for Dublin. On his arrival there he sought and obtained an interview with Mr Labouchere, Chief Secretary for Ireland, who gave him a sympathetic hearing. Doubtless in this interview, as in a public letter to the Secretary, Fr Comyn advocated the building of a railway between Kilrush and Kilkee, pointing out that it would be of more general and lasting benefit than the levelling of insignificant hills and the making of new roads which could well be dispensed with.

It may well have been Fr Comyn's suggestions which made Trevelyan at this time think over the possibility of constructing railways as a famine relief work. In a long letter to Mr Labouchere on 6 October he pointed out that there were many objections, which he enumerated, and that therefore such a scheme was not a practical possibility. Four months later Lord George Bentinck proposed a bill in Parliament to spend £16 million on railways in Ireland. It was defeated.

No relief works could begin until all the necessary formalities had been gone through and the projects approved. The first presentment sessions were not held until 4 September, and that for Moyarta barony took place after the middle of the month. A number of projects, costing £5,700, were recommended for Kilfearagh parish. These included the completion of the protecting wall on the west side of the town of Kilkee and a road around the bay in front of the lodges. The Board of Works was then asked for its approval.

Unfortunately, just at this time presentment sessions were being held all over the country and the Board of Works was literally swamped with applications. Furthermore, as no immediate local contributions had to be made and as nobody was held directly responsible for paying back the government loan, the result was what Mrs Woodham Smith has described as 'an orgy of wild extravagance'. For Kilfearagh parish alone the sum sought was about four times that approved in the previous year. And as the Board of Works, with its poor office facilities and small staff, tried to sort things out, the beginning of the actual works was held up.

In early October the application from Moyarta barony was considered by the Board of Works, and out of a sum of £25,484 applied for only £1,158 was granted. This was so ridiculously low as to be valueless. As a result it was reviewed a month later, and finally £10,077 was granted. The new decision was a big improvement on the first one, but, in the meantime, over a month had slipped by – a month in which the people were kept waiting while they grow increasingly impatient.

In late September an unexpected storm again reduced the Kilkee fishermen to desperate straits. As the sea rose, four of them went out in their canoe in a despairing effort to save their nets. At first it looked as if they might succeed because they managed to haul the nets into the boat. However, they had scarcely finished doing this when the sea claimed boat, nets and fishermen. A fund was immediately opened for the relief of the twenty-six dependents of the four drowned men. Twenty nets belonging to other fishermen were either lost or destroyed in the same storm.

As the days of October slipped by and there was still no sign of immediate employment, the people grew more and more anxious. On 11 October, Captain Mann reported that the better class of farmers had a few potatoes remaining, but the common cottiers and the labourers were, in most cases, without any. Potatoes were selling at 6*d.* a stone (three times the usual price), Indian meal at 1*s.* 9*d.* to 1*s* 10*d.* a stone and all other food in proportion. Normally the poor had their own little gardens and got some employment digging the potatoes of the larger farmers – this year there was little of either. And he went on: 'They are very patient in my immediate neighbourhood, I may say all my district for relief purposes, as yet, and I hope will continue so.' The situation was bad, but it would have been worse if many of the people had not large quantities of cured fish, which were to be a big help in the hungry winter months which followed.

Few have inexhaustible patience, particularly when they are starving. About the middle of October a meeting of the new Relief Committee was held in Kilkee Courthouse, where it was resolved to memorial the Lord Lieutenant for the immediate commencement of the works. Hundreds of poor unemployed filled the courthouse, 'their haggard appearance testifying their destitute state'. And on the 22nd of the month a large number of people from the surrounding parishes gathered in Kilrush, again for the purpose of demanding employment. Two days later a public meeting was held in the Courthouse, Ennis, to deal with the problems facing the country, and Fr Comyn was among the attendance.

In the meantime the Kilkee Relief Committee had petitioned the Commissariat Relief Office for the re-establishment of a food depot at Kilkee. The reasons for the request were outlined by the Revd J. Martin. The price of food was 'becoming every hour higher and will soon be so high that not only the labouring poor but the people generally will be unable to purchase'. If a depot were formed – even though it did not make sales – it would at least be a check. The reply received showed that the Government was going to give no help in bringing down food prices from their very high level:

> Commissary-General Sir Randolph J. Routh begs to inform you that the establishment of a depot for the sale of food in Kilkee, which you recommend, would not effect the object you have mainly in view, the reduction of prices below the market rates, as, wherever a depot is opened, the latter must rule the sales; this course being indispensable for securing the intervention of trade, without which, the public wants cannot be supplied, as it is not practicable for the Government to supply food for the whole population; and it cannot be expected that trade competition could intervene if prices were to be adopted at the depots which would not enable traders selling at the same rates to realize their reasonable profits ...

Sometime after this, however, Captain Mann did succeed in getting permission to make sales from the Kilrush depot at a price which forced the big wholesale merchants to lower their prices, and, in late November, it was decided to issue meal to Kilkee Relief Committee.

WORKING ON THE ROADS

At the very end of October or in early November relief work finally began – even though the projected works had not yet got final approval from the Board of Works. In Kilkee 750 men were employed and the task of making a road and footpath around the bay was begun. Within days the numbers employed on relief works in Clare reached fantastic proportions – 23,899 on 8 November, reckoned as one in three of the able-bodied male population and far higher than the number employed in any other county. However, in the extreme west of Clare public employment was needed not just for a third of the able-bodied but certainly for well over two-thirds, and at a meeting in Carrigaholt on 3 November for the parishes of Kilfearagh, Moyarta and Kilballyowen, dissatisfaction was expressed at several aspects of the working of the relief scheme. It was pointed out that the rate of wages, 8*d.* per day, would require nine days' work from a man in order to enable him to buy two stone of meal at the then current rate of 2*s.* 10*d.* to 3*s.* per stone. This amount of meal for nine days would not even provide as much daily for the average family as they would later get under outdoor relief.

The insufficiency of the wages was also noted by two members of the Society of Friends, James Harvey and Thomas Grubb, who visited West Clare in early 1847. They remarked in their report that families were by this time entirely dependent on the wages received from the roadworks and that generally only one person from each family could get employment. Their report continued:

> Indeed, their week's wage, when exchanged for food, is not more than sufficient for three or four days' consumption. They endeavour, however, to stretch it over the week; but it is no uncommon thing with many families to be without any food for twenty-four or thirty-six hours before the succeeding pay day comes round, with the exception of the man or boy who is at work. To prevent his strength (upon which all their living depends) from failing, the scanty subsistence of the others is still further reduced, to provide him with sufficient to sustain him. So pressing are the calls of hunger that when the week's supply of meal is brought home (perhaps a distance of six miles) it is in many cases eaten before it is fully cooked; some bake it on a griddle; but among the very poorest, and where the family is large, in order to make it go far it is boiled into gruel. Is it then to be wondered that

dysentery, the general result of insufficient and imperfectly cooked food, should be, as it is, so prevalent among them?

Insufficient food was not the only cause of hardship for the roadworkers. It was a cold winter, and they were not used to working in the open at this time of the year. As a result they were poorly clothed in face of the icy gales. Captain Mann wrote: 'I always considered that from the beginning of December to February, the suffering from weather, want of food and clothing was the severest and past [*sic*] any description of mine – causing afterwards the sad effects from disease.' And even where labourers had some clothing at the beginning of winter, this eventually went into pawn. The result, in the words of Dr Griffin, was that 'the poor people go literally half naked to their work and sleep at night without changing their clothes, having no other night covering'. It was little wonder, then, that fever and other sicknesses soon began to wreak havoc.

One result of the relief employment was that farm work was neglected, even though Captain Wynne, Inspecting Officer for West Clare, tried to reduce the numbers on the works and get the people back to their farms. At the end of November Captain H.D. Hutchinson, Inspecting Officer for Clare, reported that in a journey of fifty-six miles he saw only one plough at work preparing the ground for wheat. And, about a month later, it was stated from Kilrush that all the small farmers in the vicinity had neglected their land as they had no seed. Unless the Government supplied this, the consequences would be serious.

In general, then, the picture was a dismal one, and there was little to relieve the gloom. However, in October, some landlords began to reduce rents, and in mid November the *Nation* began to publish lists of landlords who were reducing or foregoing rents. One such was Lord Conyngham. In early November it was reported that he had instructed his agent, Marcus Keane, to reduce the rents on his Clare estate by twenty-five per cent and fifteen per cent according to the circumstances of the tenantry.

CLOSE OF THE YEAR

Although elsewhere in Clare there were disturbances of various kinds, Kilfearagh remained quiet. But it was only a surface calm. In early November the following notice was found at Doonbeg Chapel and probably at Kilkee also:

> Notice is hereby given, to the needy and distressed in this parish, to assemble on Monday at the Kilrush Workhouse in order to be admitted themselves and their families, and if refused, to be willing to

commit depredations, slaughter cattle, open stores and farmers' yards, before they die of hunger.

N.B. One of these is sent to every parish in the union.

Later in the month the Kilrush Board of Guardians sent a memorial to Lord John Russell suggesting assisted emigration as the best method of tackling Ireland's problems:

We do not hesitate to suggest, that every great feature leading to, or now exhibited by the present crisis, points to an extensive system of emigration, as the remedy not only best adapted to relieve the distress of this land, but also to become a means of increasing our Empire, by reclaiming to the use of man, some of the large uncultivated tracts of our colonies.

Perhaps they already had some premonition of the pressure which was soon to be put on their own resources – but, then, no premonition was needed. One had only to look at the actual condition of the people. On 5 December Captain Wynne wrote:

In the Barony of Moyarta Mr Marcus Keane, a gentleman of high character, has investigated and ascertained at my instance the state of the several townlands and parishes and it is truly deplorable; including the remnant of the potato crop, there are not provisions for three weeks and these too in the hands of a few individuals; now at the expiration of this period all the money in the Treasury cannot meet the wants of the frightful population in that district without importing provisions.

And three weeks later he added:

Without food we cannot last many days longer; the Public Works must fail in keeping the population alive. What is to become of the thousands to whose cases the Relief Works are totally inapplicable? The Relief Committees have not a shilling; they cannot, or will not, pay even for stationery and postage. I am obliged to pay these expenses; therefore nothing is to be expected from them.

Soup Kitchens and Deaths from Starvation

As the old year closed so did the new year open. Cold, hunger and disease now went hand in hand. On 4 January, the *Clare Journal* wrote: 'The state of this country is becoming every day more alarming ... Gaunt famine has already spread her sable wings over the land ...' And three days later if commented: 'Throughout the entire extent of this county destitution prevails to a frightful extent but perhaps in no part of it is the condition of the people more painfully distressing than in Kilkee and the surrounding country.'

It was not surprising, then, that in the early days of January a deputation consisting of Henry S. Burton, the Revd Mr Martin, the Revd M. Duggan, PP, Carrigaholt, and Fr Comyn went to Dublin to request further employment for the poor of their district. When they met Mr Labouchere, the Chief Secretary, they pointed out that in their area the proportion of the destitute employed on public works was no more than one in 7½. Those employed had been seen staggering through weakness while at work, and, according to the stewards, hundreds of them were never seen to taste food from morning to nightfall. The people had pawned their very day clothes and night-covering and, after a hard day's work, had to lie down at night on a bed of straw without a blanket or coverlet of any kind. In Kilkee oatmeal now cost 5s. per stone – far too dear for the ordinary people. In fact there were so many destitute in the area that it would cost £1,500 a week to provide them with one meal a day. The deputation also recommended the reclaiming of 20,000 acres of bog in the district of Kilfearagh and Killard. In doing this they probably had particularly in mind the memorial of the Kilrush Board of Guardians to Lord John Russell regarding emigration, as they urged that people should be located on the waste lands in preference to the colonial lands.

Mr Labouchere referred the deputation to Colonel Jones and Sir Randolph Routh. The latter asked that local subscriptions be immediately collected but was reminded that Mr Burton himself was the only resident landlord in a district of twenty-six miles. Nevertheless, Routh continued to insist on an attempt being made to collect money, promising a grant equal to the amount donated. Such a promise was of doubtful value, as local subscriptions would almost inevitably be quite small. However, the deputation did not go away empty-handed, as they also got an assurance that instructions would be given for increased employment in the area.

Fr Comyn next turned to the Duke of Leinster and in a letter asked him to use his influence with the Central Relief Committee of Ireland to get a grant for the starving poor of his parishes. Here his efforts were successful, for shortly afterwards it was reported that the General Central Relief Committee had given him £60, while he got another £20 from the Indian Relief Committee. The Revd Mr Martin also got £20 from the latter committee, as well as the gift of a boiler.

SOUP KITCHENS

The gift of the boiler by the Indian Relief Committee is indicative of the new trend being taken by relief efforts – and not just by private organisations but by the Government also. On 25 January, Lord John Russell outlined his latest proposals in the House of Commons:

1. For the third time since the first failure of the potato crop, new relief committees were to be nominated by the Lord Lieutenant, and these were to be given the duty of establishing soup kitchens which would feed the people without any work being required in return.

2. The purpose of the free distribution of soup was 'that labouring men should be allowed to work on their own plots of ground, or for the farmers, and thus tend to produce food for the next harvest and procure perhaps some small wages to enable them to support their families.' Consequently, as the distribution of food became general, the public works would be gradually closed and would not be re-started.

3. Although it had been a fundamental principle of the Irish Poor Law system that nobody received relief unless he became an inmate of a workhouse, this was now to be changed. Under the new proposed legislation, paupers would be given outdoor relief, to be paid for out of the local rates, and in fact the Soup Kitchen Act was only intended as a temporary measure to feed the people until the necessary legislative and other steps had been taken to provide outdoor relief at the workhouses. It was not until four months later that the Irish Poor Law Extension bill permitting outdoor relief was finally passed and it became law on 8 June. Meanwhile the Soup Kitchen Act was in operation, having become law on 26 February.

In the meantime, before Lord John Russell's official proclamation of his Soup Kitchen policy in Parliament, the deputation from Kilfearagh and other West Clare parishes had returned home from Dublin. Immediately a soup kitchen was established, with official approval, and placed under the management of a committee consisting of Jonas Studdert, Fr Comyn, Dr John Griffin, and Thomas Parker. Francis O'Donnell was treasurer and the Revd J. Martin secretary. It was decided that, pending the arrival of the promised boiler from Dublin, use would be made of the boilers which heated water for the Baths. The new soup kitchen was to be supported by monthly donations – seemingly promised by individuals – and any donations received otherwise. They also had the promise made by Routh of matching any local donations from government funds. Quite possibly the £5 which Fr Comyn received from Dr Kennedy, Bishop of Killaloe, in mid-February for the relief of the poor, was also used for this purpose. Commenting on the establishment of the soup kitchen the *Limerick Chronicle* remarked that the destitution in Kilkee was very great, as many poor people followed the summer visitors to the town and then, by easily getting lodgings in winter, remained as a permanent burden on the locality.

Under the provisions of the Soup Kitchen Act a new relief committee had to be formed in Kilkee, as the one supervising the soup kitchen in early spring had been formed before the act came into effect. This new committee held its first meeting in early April. Its activities, however, were not confined to doling out soup. It was entitled to distribute meal also and to issue ration cards stating the amount of food to which the holder was entitled.

But the relief committee was not the only source from which the people received help. The Society of Friends frequently sent gifts of money, food and clothing during 1847 and following years, as did many private individuals. The gifts of clothing were channelled through the Ladies' Clothing Society at Kilkee, which seems to have done a good deal to keep the people decently clothed.

DEATHS FROM STARVATION AND FEVER

As winter changed into spring, deaths began to be recorded from starvation. A Kilkee correspondent wrote to the *Limerick Reporter* in late February:

> I am sorry to inform you that Kilkee, I fear, will soon be a second Skibbereen, the starving poor day after day falling off the works, and dying. A poor man named Blood ... was found prostrate on the road, having thrown up a large quantity of blood, and, in a short time after, he expired. This untimely end the poor man declared to be the effects of starvation. Many others, it is to be apprehended, will meet the same fate in this locality. God only knows when and where it will stop.

And there were many others: *Limerick Chronicle*, 6 February – 'An inquest was held on Sunday last in Kilkee on the body of a poor man who died on his way to the workhouse, Kilrush'; *Limerick Chronicle*, 27 March – 'A poor man fell dead of cold and starvation at Moyarta.' But the very fact that individual deaths were being reported shows such happenings were not so frequent as no longer to arouse comment.

Fever now began to sweep the country. At the beginning of March the Kilrush Workhouse had 1,100–1,200 inmates, even though it had been built originally to cope with only 800. Fever was rampant; nearly a quarter of the inmates were sick, and the master, his daughter and the doctor were down with fever. The guardians, with a few exceptions, were afraid to go near it through fear of disease. The fever hospital, built originally for thirty-six patients, had forty-eight at the beginning of March, but the mortality rate does not appear to have been particularly high. However, the worst of the fever epidemic had not yet come. In the country in general it reached its climax in April but did not begin to subside until September. Describing the situation in Moyarta barony in July, Fr Michael Meehan, CC Kilrush, said that about every tenth family was in actual fever:

> There are, and have been all the summer, hovels in this barony and in every parish of it, where the sick were obliged to grope and totter to the door for turf, water, meal, etc., which a charitable neighbour would bring to the threshold and no further – the only friend that would enter there was the Priest.

The town of Kilkee seems to have fared somewhat better than the surrounding countryside. In late June it was reported to be free from disease.

Fr Meehan also gives us a glimpse of a priest's work at this time. With reference to the priests of Moyarta barony he wrote:

> Most of the priests have ten or twelve calls per day, and must ride twenty or thirty miles to take them in. The physician and the humane *may* go to *some* with temporal relief; the poor Priest *must* go to *all* with the consolations of his ministry. And, indeed, not the least of our hardships is that, exploring the most thrilling abodes of distress, we have not wherewithal to make our corporal works of mercy commensurate with the spiritual.

It was against this background that emigration began to appear as the only way of escape. On 18 March the *Clare Journal* reported: 'Emigration from all parts of this country is now taking place to a most unprecedented extent.' In Kilfearagh parish the numbers leaving would not, as yet, be very great, though it was stated that in Kilkee many were trying to dispose of their farms and lodges so that they could begin life anew on the other side of the Atlantic.

PREPARING FOR THE NEW HARVEST

On 16 March, Captain Mann wrote: 'As yet, except among the strong farmers, tillage is very much neglected.' Four days later the first reduction in numbers of the public works took place, and further reductions took place at intervals after that. Although the purpose of this was to leave the labourers free to till the fields, the hoped-for result was not achieved. On 24 March the *Limerick Chronicle* reported that there was no sign of the land being worked in the vicinity of Kilkee, and there was no immediate improvement in the situation. There were several reasons for this lack of preparation:

1. After two successive failures of the potato crop, many felt that there was little point in sowing potatoes. It was known that in America the potatoes had failed in three successive years.

2. The conacre system had virtually come to an end. In 1846 nobody who had let out land on conacre had received any rent, and as a result the owners were now inclined to keep it themselves for grass and cattle. In any case, quite probably nobody would be inclined to take land on conacre, even if it was available.

3. There was a widespread shortage of potato seed and, indeed, of seed of any kind. In many cases what had at first been kept for this purpose was eventually wholly or partly eaten as food. In March a supply of bere and rye seed arrived in Kilrush and was sold by Captain Mann – but not without difficulty, only 'by dent of persuasion and having it published by the RC clergy'. The rye was to prove particularly successful. During the winter a supply of it had arrived at the Kilrush depot from Russia and it had become quite popular with the poor. Now a considerable amount was sown in West Clare – where it could be planted on inferior land – and was to prove a good substitute for the potato when harvested.

Captain Mann's difficulty in disposing of the seed may seem strange at first sight. But there was a simple explanation. The Government at one stage intended to advance £50,000 to landlords to enable them to purchase and distribute seed to their tenants. The seed merchants objected, and as the plan might interfere with private enterprise it was withdrawn. However, in March and early April the farmers in West Clare were still hopeful of receiving free seed and therefore were very reluctant to purchase. On 12 April HMS *Dragon* brought another supply of seed to Kilrush. A little was purchased by a few landlords and then the ship sailed away again with most of its cargo. It was only at this stage that it finally dawned on the people that they were not going to get any free seed, and Captain Mann was now besieged with applications for seed of any kind. A few days later a steamer arrived with a cargo of oat seed, and the greater part of it was immediately purchased and sown. 'A sudden and favourable reaction took place, all appearing anxious to till something, and not let the land run to waste.'

About the same time a large amount of turnip seed was imported by local dealers in West Clare, and those who could, bought and tilled it. Then, at the end of May, Sir R. Routh found that he had 40,000 lbs. of turnip and green crop seed left on his hands and he gave them to the Society of Friends for free distribution. A small quantity of the turnip seed was received by Captain Mann for distribution in his district.

The final result of the spring sowing was the amount of potatoes planted was very much smaller than usual. On the other hand, a vast increase had taken place in the acreage under turnips. In County Clare as a whole only 6,129 acres were planted with potatoes in 1847, whereas 10,968 were planted with turnips. Such a change about would have seemed incredible even two years previously, but it was to have some beneficial results. In the following winter the turnips were to save many lives, as Twisleton noted on 25 January 1848, when he wrote:

> The gratuitous distribution of the turnip seed last year I believe saved more lives than almost anything else.

One final point about the spring work must be noted. By the beginning of June, little turf had been cut near Poulnasherry for the Limerick trade. This was to mean a big income loss to the area.

SUMMER 1847

The summer season at Kilkee opened on a rather ominous note. The theft of a quantity of meal from the local relief depot became a minor matter when the body of a murdered woman, a visitor to Kilkee, was found in a bog about two miles from the town. The police immediately fixed their suspicions on a man named Ryan, who, like the murdered woman, was from Hospital, County Limerick. When they visited the house where he had been staying he had fled, but they discovered the stolen meal in a bed-tick. Three weeks later Daniel Ryan was arrested by Head Constable John Mullarchy of Kilrush and charged with murder. His motive was thought to be a desire to get possession of a few pounds the poor woman was reputed to have.

Even when reporting the murder incident the *Limerick Chronicle* hastened to assure its readers that, despite the destitution, there had been no outrage or plunder at Kilkee. And, as we have already mentioned, the town was free from fever. A month later a correspondent of the *Limerick Reporter* painted an even brighter picture:

> I have much pleasure to announce to the visitors who frequent this much admired watering-place, that the people, as usual, are most peaceable, and that new potatoes are now exposed for sale at the low price of 8*d*. per stone, perfectly sound and free from disease, notwith-

standing the prognostications of the black prophets of the west. Vegetables are plenty [*sic*], and our markets are well supplied with beef and mutton at 5*d*. per lb., and our village presenting a gay appearance already. Wheat and barley are doing very well, but the oat crop is rather deficient. Many of our poor natives have suffered rather severely during this trying season, which they bore with that patient endurance characteristic of the Irish peasant.

In mid-August Kilkee was stated to be more crowded than it had ever been – but soon afterwards the season ended prematurely. And to add to the people's losses the potato crop, such as it was, was by no means the healthy one expected in July.

END OF PUBLIC WORKS AND SOUP KITCHENS

As we have seen, the soup kitchens were to tide the people over the gap between the gradual winding up of the public works and the coming into operation of outdoor relief. At first a closing date of 15 August was fixed for the soup kitchens, but the extreme want in many areas, especially in the south and south-west and probably including Kilkee, caused some delay. However, 1 October was definitely fixed as the last day for the distribution of rations in any union through the soup kitchens.

By this time the public works had also been wound up – a process which had been virtually completed by the end of June – and the Government was quite determined not to restart them. Nevertheless, in late September, a memorial from the 'Clergy, Gentry and Inhabitants of Kilkee' was presented to the Lord Lieutenant, complaining of the unfinished state of the sea-wall and other public works and stating that all of what had been done in Kilkee would be swept away by the high tides of winter unless completed before then. A few weeks later a deputation from Clare called on the Lord Lieutenant and asked for a loan for the re-commencement of public works already begun and incomplete. The answer held out no hope: 'We understand that his Excellency, while he deplored the wretched state into which the country had been plunged, held out no hope that the prayer of the Memorial, so far as related to a loan of money, could be granted.' Still exploring every avenue, Fr Comyn wrote to Henry Grattan, MP, at the end of October, with a view to having the situation in the Kilkee area brought before the notice of the Irish MPs at a meeting to be held shortly afterwards. All in vain. The public works and the soup kitchens were now very definitely a thing of the past and West Clare was thrown back on its own resources – with terrible results.

Towards Utter Destitution

CAUSES OF DESTITUTION

Looking back at the suffering of the previous twelve months Captain Mann wrote on 15 November 1847:

> A great deal has been written and many an account given of the dreadful sufferings endured by the poor. Believe me, my dear Sir, the reality in most cases far exceeded description. Indeed none can conceive what it was but those who were in it. For my part I frequently look back on it as a fearful and horrid dream, scarcely knowing how to sufficiently express gratitude to the Almighty for having brought the country through it even as it is.

Mann was correct in assuming that a chapter had closed, but he appears to have been totally unaware that a new and more terrible one was opening. There were several reasons for the increased destitution. The cessation or near-cessation of conacre had meant that the poorest section of the population had no supply of food for the winter. Those who had planted potatoes were caught by the new failure, and, as we shall see, even those who formerly were a little above subsistence level were caught between the rival claims of the rent and rate collectors. In November 'A Looker-On, Kilkee' wrote:

> Last year the poor had pigs and potatoes, such as they were. The pigs are gone, and the small quantity of potatoes remaining from this year's crop are rapidly becoming diseased. I know a respectable person who, in the last fortnight, lost ten barrels out of fourteen ... The grain food is rapidly disappearing ... It has been officially stated that rents were never better paid than this year. In many instances it is true; but it is equally so that the majority of those who have been thus punctual, were so through fear of being turned out of the ground; and I know of several who, after paying their rents, are without any means of supporting their families. Throughout the whole district it is one scene of misery and distress; the paupers are starving notwithstanding the poor law; and the other classes are but a few degrees removed from them. Every available article is either sold or in pawn, even to the very beds and blankets; and no man can assist his neighbour as heretofore.

In place of the public works and soup kitchens the people now had to turn to the workhouse for their salvation, and it can be truly said that from this time on the story of the people of Kilfearagh parish becomes centred more and more on Kilrush Workhouse. Under the Poor Law Extension Act of 1847 it was possible now to grant outdoor relief, that is, the workhouses could give food to people who were not inmates. But normally this relief would be given only to the destitute who were aged or infirm, widows or children. The able-bodied would receive relief only within the workhouses – as otherwise it was feared that the scheme would be unworkable because of the number of applicants. However, outdoor relief to the able-bodied could be given if the Poor Law Commissioners issued an order authorising it.

Practically all this new and heavy expense would have to be paid for out of the poor law rates collected locally – although Kilrush Union did get some help from the Government, being classified as 'distressed'. Already, in many places, quite a lot of difficulty had been experienced in collecting, and the burden was now far greater. It had also some side-effects. Landlords were liable for the rates on holdings valued at £4 and under, and this was true even though the rent had not been paid. To avoid the rates, the cabin had to be pulled down. It is no coincidence, then, that the beginning of the mass evictions in Kilrush Union coincided with the coming into operation of the new system of relief. Furthermore, a clause in the new act, known as the 'quarter-acre clause' or 'Gregory clause', aided the landlords in this process. Under this provision no relief was granted to the family of a man who held a quarter acre of ground or more. He had the choice, then, of keeping his farm and getting no relief or giving up his farm and entering the workhouse. Indeed, the position with regard to this clause was such that Twisleton could write on 13 January 1848:

> It would seem ... that a Relieving Officer cannot give relief, even in cases of starvation, to anyone who occupies more than a quarter of an acre of land.

The increased rates spurred the landlords on to evictions. But the farmer with a valuation of a little over £4 was almost the hardest hit of all. Before 1845 these would have been reasonably comfortable by Irish standards. Now they were hit on all sides – the landlord competing with the rate collector to see who would get his payment. Trevelyan even asked: 'Is there no power of securing the rates out of the produce of the crops seized for rent?' Seemingly there was not. Writing from Kilrush Union on 11 November, Captain Kennedy, the newly appointed Poor Law Inspector, stated that a major mistake had been committed with regard to the issue of the warrant for collection of rates in the union. If it had been done a month earlier, the rate collectors would have arrived before the crops were swept by the landlords or sold by the tenants. And a week later he wrote:

> Empty walls, an iron pot and children in swarms are all I can see or the collector find. In some lawless localities, I expect resistance, but in these places they are able to pay; the law being vigorously put in force with a few, will, I trust, decide the matter ... I hope for the countenance of the RC clergy in the collection of this most righteous impost.

And it was little wonder that many were unwilling to pay the poor rate. In 1845 it had been 10*d*. in Kilkee Electoral Division. By 1846 it had gone up to 1*s*. 3*d*. and in 1847 it soared to 6*s*. 10*d*. Combined with a Grand Jury rate of 3*s*. 10*d*. this meant that 10*s*. 8*d*. had to be paid on each £1 valuation. Some statistics supplied by the Poor Law offices explain the rising costs, keeping in mind also the cessation of government aid. In 1845 the proportion of people relieved by the poor law in Kilfearagh parish was one in 238. In 1846 it was one in 102. By 1847 it was one in twenty-nine and, continuing the rapidly worsening position, in 1848 it was one in three and in 1849 one in two.

As destitution spread it moved from the labourer to the small farmer and eventually even to those who had been quite comfortable in 1845. In 1851 we can find a notice like the following in the obituary column of the *Limerick Reporter and Tipperary Vindicator.*

> At Kilrush Workhouse, Martin Haren, formerly a respectable farmer.

In the face of all this, the efforts of individuals could no longer do anything to achieve results like those got by Fr Comyn, the Revd Mr Martin, Hugh Hogan and others in 1845-6 and for most of 1847. These now move completely into the background as the Guardians and officials of Kilrush Workhouse take the centre of the stage. For two years after the first appearance of the blight the old way of life had been held tenuously together. In the months and years after autumn 1847 it gradually disintegrated.

AUTUMN AND WINTER 1847-8

In mid-October three fishermen were drowned at Farrihy, the first of a number of such accidents in this part of the parish over a period of a few years. Just as most men had for long been unfit to work on the roads or elsewhere, so too the fishermen had not the stamina required for fishing. Fr Meehan wrote of the fishermen in Moyarta barony:

This year they were not able to fish; for each canoe (light boats made of laths and tarred canvass) required three men to fish effectively, and these should row, while fishing, about ten miles. This length of rowing in our very rough seas required strength and agility, which had fled from the skin and bones frames of our poor fishermen this year.

By early 1848 the fishermen were absolutely destitute. It was claimed that the fish had gone from the coast and there was nothing to catch. Their nets had once again been brought to the pawnshop, and, although worth £1 each, only 5s. had been given for them. The simple truth was that even at this low price the pawnbrokers could not get buyers – because very few were fishing. In the district along the coast from Tarbert Island to Black Head there were 676 boats employing 2,393 men and boys registered with the coastguards on 1 January 1846. On 1 January 1848 the figures for the same area were eleven vessels and forty men. Yet, despite their great hardships, Captain Kennedy found that the fishermen, as a class, were very slow to enter the workhouse – seemingly even much slower than others.

In November 1847 Mr Walsh, an agricultural instructor sent by Lord Clarendon and the Royal Agricultural Society of Ireland, was deputed by the Guardians of Kilrush Union to deliver a lecture in Kilkee. Mr Walsh was especially concerned with drainage, the use of manure and the encouragement of the growing of flax. But by this time something more than mere advice was needed. If, nearly two years previously, the people had been merely 'half-starved' in the Irish sense of the term, they were now 'starved'. In the neighbourhood of Kilkee men, women and children were to be seen rooting up the potato fields, already dug, in the hope of finding a few stray potatoes which had been previously overlooked. On 25 November Captain Kennedy wrote:

> The north and west of the union, including the divisions Kilmurry, Killard, Kilmacduane, Kilkee and a part of Moyarta, are in a most lamentable state. The parts on the coast are most densely populated, with a turf-digging, seaweed gathering, fishing-catching, amphibious population; as bad fishermen as they are agriculturalists. They have no regular mode of gaining a livelihood ... A few acres of reclaimed bog planted with potatoes has heretofore supplied their wants, and rendered them content on the lowest possible scale of existence. While westerly gales prevail during the winter, large numbers eke out a wretched existence gathering seaweed, which they carry and sell further inland for manure. The villages of Mullagh, Doonbeg, Bealaha and Kilkee are wretched nests of filth, famine and disease.

Captain Kennedy went on to say that the whole district seemed swept of food, and he reckoned that one-third of the population would be without food at Christmas, two-thirds starving before February and the whole without food or money before May.

In Kilkee some of the lodge-owners were quite well off, but the remainder were every bit as badly circumstanced as their country brethren. In the out-skirts of the town a special reporter of the *Limerick and Clare Examiner* saw scenes of 'unparallelled wretchedness'. 'God alone know how they are to get over the winter; I fear much, it will be a winter of death for many of them.' A short distance from the town, on his way to Carrigaholt, he saw eighty acres which had been left untilled for want of seed. Inquiring about this he was told:

> It wasn't tilling we were thinking of, but the hunger – we had nothing to put in it. When the famine came, they died, as the birds do, when the frost comes, and what we thought we never would see, they were buried without the coffin.

Burial without a coffin was the ultimate sign of destitution – and with the coffin disappeared most of the funeral ritual so dear to the people. Fever was now raging, and in some localities in West Clare cases of smallpox also occurred. As a result, funerals, which had formerly been attended by great throngs of people, had become smaller and smaller. The frequency of their occurrence and fear of infection reduced the number of mourners to a group barely sufficient to carry the coffin to the grave and bury it – if there was a coffin. Many corpses, perhaps half of those now being buried in West Clare, were wrapped in straw and swathed around with a sugawn. And Captain Kennedy met one poor man carrying his two dead children to the grave in a cradle. Needless to remark, wakes had become rare occurrences. During most of 1847 Kilrush Workhouse provided a large number of coffins for people who were not inmates – but even here the contractor was unpaid in early November and threatening to stop supplies. And in this same month the Poor Law Commissioners informed Boards of Guardians that they were not to provide coffins for those who did not die in the workhouse.

From late 1847 onwards, then, many people entered the workhouse for the sole purpose of getting what they considered to be a decent burial. In February 1851, Dr Madden, historian of the United Irishmen, visited Kilrush Workhouse and described a crowd seeking admission as follows:

> These sick and famishing creatures were brought there, as I was informed, by neighbours who had lent cars to carry them to the Poorhouse, and a great number of them, to use their own language, 'for a coffin'. On surprise being expressed at hearing this reason given

for the removal of these people, and the question being repeated, one of those moribund applicants for admission in order to get a shell and a grave, – a man more like a skeleton than a living man, yet not much above forty years of age – said in a low hollow-toned voice – 'Yes, to get a coffin, your honour.'

The type of burial they got, however, hardly made their visit to the workhouse worthwhile. Again to quote Dr Madden:

> The dead are interred every morning in a churchyard (Shanakyle) about a mile and half from the town. The bodies are carted away without any appearance of a funeral ceremony; no attendance of priest or parson, no pall. The coffins – if the frail boards nailed together for the remains of paupers may be so called – are made by contract, and furnished 'at a very low figure'. The paupers' trench in a corner of the churchyard, which I visited, is a large pit, the yawning aperture about twenty feet square. The dead are deposited in layers, and over each coffin a little earth is thinly scattered, just sufficient to conceal the boards. The thickness of the covering of clay I found did not amount to two inches over the last tier of coffins deposited there. A pauper who drives the cart, and another who accompanies him to assist in taking the coffins from that conveyance, and slipping them down into the trench, are the only funeral attendants. It is very rare that any of the kith or kin of a pauper accompany his remains to the grave, because there are so many deaths, and so much difficulty in ascertaining anything about the identity of such a multitude of paupers as those amounting to half a hundred or more who die in a week, that it is seldom anything is known of the deaths in the Poorhouse by the friends outside, if any there be left, until long after they have taken place.

The charge was also made that those who had a shirt were not even given a shroud. It was this final indignity which prompted an anonymous writer to contribute some verses to the *Nation*:

> Aye, buried like dogs are the Poor-house Dead
> In this Christian land, without shroud or shred
> Of a winding sheet on the wasted frame –
> And this Godless thrift is our Guardians' aim!
> No prayer for the Dead, to offend the ear
> Of our Saxon 'Saints' is repeated here;
> Of 'mummeries', none that 'degrade the mind'
> And debase the soul, in Kilrush you'll find.

Thus did many of the people of Kilfearagh parish go to their final resting place.

If deaths were on the increase, marriages were on the decrease. In 1840, 104 marriages from Kilfearagh and Killard parishes were entered into the register at Kilkee Catholic Church. In 1846 the number was 106, well up to and perhaps even above the average of the previous decade. But in 1847 this had dropped to 36 (19 of them with addresses in Kilfearagh parish) and in the two years 1848-9 there were only 41 in all. The reduction in the number of marriages and the general straitened circumstances of his flock caused a serious drop in Fr Comyn's income. Perhaps his charitable efforts too, contributed to his having to leave his house and farm on the outskirts of Kilkee and go into lodgings in the town.

By 18 November 1847 over 6,000 notices to quit had been served in Kilrush Union, and Kilfearagh parish was no different in this respect from the others. The land under ejectment was literally bare of all stock and produce. Little wonder, then, that the *Limerick Chronicle* could write in mid December of the Kilkee area: 'The people, we have heard, are one half starving, the other half plundering.' A threatening notice against Jonas Studdert and two others, which was signed 'Molly Maguire', was found on the door of Kilkee Protestant church one Sunday morning, while armed bands were seen on different occasions on the road between Kilkee and Doonbeg. On 14 December Captain Mann wrote: 'Hitherto we have been most quiet and outrage has been unknown, but I do fear we shall not always be so. There is undoubted reason to think that there are some ruffians lurking about in the vicinity of Kilkee and Killard who are on a mischievous errand. The police are using every exertion to find them out and occasionally get on their track.' Soon afterwards the number of soldiers in Kilrush was increased.

As 1848 opened, robberies became more frequent occurrences. At the beginning of January two women were committed to Ennis Gaol for stealing tea, sugar, powder and shot from a milk-can left in front of a Kilkee public-house. In February Miss Fahy, mistress of the National School at Kilkee, returned home from school one evening to find that she had been robbed of £20 and her clothes. A fortnight later Mr Hogan's grocery store was broken into at night. However, when seen against the general background of want these happenings become more understandable.

The traders, or at least many of them, were now reaping the reward of government non-intervention, and the people were utterly at their mercy. In January the *Limerick Chronicle* reported that the greatest imposition was generally practised by traders in West Clare, and on 1 March Captain Kennedy wrote:

I know that a description of Indian meal, hardly fit for human food, is retailed at an immense profit through the Union, and that the retailers have realised very large sums.

Advantage, too, was being taken of the very many men who were ready to grasp any opportunity of obtaining work. Captain Mann commented on 11 February:

> Employment there is none and I am sorry to say it is stated and with truth that the farmers are in many instances taking advantage of this state of things and getting their work done for the man's diet and perhaps a little tobacco, thus leaving the wife and children no share.

RELIEF ORGANISATIONS

When a man had no means of supporting his wife and children, they generally had eventually to face towards the workhouse. Some, however, were supported through help from charitable organisations. We have already seen that in 1847 the Society of Friends commenced sending donations and gifts to relieve distress in Kilfearagh parish. Such help continued to arrive during 1848, probably increasing in volume. In January the Revd James Martin acknowledged the receipt of twelve barrels of Indian meal and one barrel of pork and a fortnight later a cwt. of rice arrived from the same source. Other gifts included bales of clothing material and bed covering.

Private individuals and firms also helped, probably after having been applied to. Mrs Driver of Peckham sent £5 for the employment of poor women in their own cabins; an anonymous Friend sent three dozen men's and boys' caps, while various people sent small money donations. In the stricken area itself few of the better off opened their purses. But, then, they had not been accustomed to doing so. In the context of West Clare, Captain Mann wrote on 13 February 1848:

> The old cant that charity was so unbounded etc. etc., is all humbug; the poor always cared for the poor – what have the rich as a body done throughout this awful visitation? – some do make a great fuss and try to beguile themselves into a belief that they are doing wonders... but what is the wondrous work? Why being very active in distributing the funds sent from various charitable institutions and trying to secure the largest amount for their own immediate dependents.

Along with the Society of Friends there was another voluntary organisation which made a very valuable contribution towards stemming the tide.

This was the British Association for the Relief of the extreme Distress in the remote Parishes of Ireland and Scotland, founded in January 1847. In early January 1848 Trevelyan told Captain Mann to make an application for aid to Count Strzelecki of the British Association. Mann followed his instructions, and the result was a grant of £100 for relief in Kilrush Union, together with a promise of £500 for the purchasing and making of children's clothes. Captain Mann was delighted at this – as it would provide a market for homemade serge together with giving employment to destitute widows. The cloth was then bought in the market at Kilrush, and a house was rented in which the clothes were made under the supervision of some local ladies. Employment was given there to 150 poor women. The end products were distributed among the poor children of the district.

Although further cash grants were made by the British Relief Association to Kilrush Union, its most important project was the provision of food for children attending National Schools in this union and elsewhere in the West of Ireland. Between 1 October 1847 and 25 April 1848, 3,362 national school children in Kilrush Union received meals. And in a five-month period from December to April (inclusive) nearly half a million meals were served. Kilkee National School shared in this bounty, which was invaluable to the children. Captain Mann commented: 'It is impossible to estimate too highly the value and importance of feeding the destitute children at the schools.'

Although only very poor children were helped in the schools by the British Association, Captain Kennedy revealed an anomaly in mid-March. In Kilkee National School the teachers demanded the payment of one penny a week from each child – and this excluded the really destitute from the school and put them outside the scope of the scheme. This was a rather awkward situation, as it was National Board policy that portion of the teachers' salaries should come from weekly contributions from the pupils. When informed of the situation in Kilkee, it ordered that children receiving British Association relief were not to be charged for instruction.

On 1 July 1848 the funds of the British Association finally dried up, but Lord John Russell promised that the relief it was giving to 200,000 school children would be kept up by the Government. But a little over two months later, despite this promise, the free distribution of food in the schools of Kilrush Union came to an end.

POLITICS

Although most people in Kilfearagh parish no longer had the intense interest in politics of five or six years earlier when O'Connell was at the height of his repeal campaign, 1848 was the year in which the political developments of the decade came to a head. In January 1847 the Young Irelanders, having earlier seceded from the Repeal Association, founded a new and militant organisation, the Irish Confederation. The plan was to found confederate clubs throughout the country to exert pressure on the Government to repeal the Act of Union. In fact, very few such clubs were founded initially. However, in May and June 1848 events swiftly moved the Young Irelanders towards an armed rebellion and an effort was made to increase the number of clubs. In early June an attempt was made to unite the Repeal Association and the Irish Confederation through the replacement of both by a new association, the Irish League. It was agreed that the confederate clubs were not to be disbanded but were to remain, the nucleus of a national guard. Gavan Duffy believed that the League would provide a means of introducing armed clubs into the rural areas where the Confederation had previously made little progress.

On 21 June Fr Comyn expressed his delight at the prospect of a reunion among Repealers and about three weeks later attended a meeting of the League in Dublin at which he was proposed for membership by Thomas D'Arcy McGee. Fr Comyn, however, was no republican revolutionary and was obviously expecting constitutional agitation. He would have little sympathy, then, with the aims of some of those who founded the Lord Clare Club in Kilkee about this same time. When the ill-fated rebellion broke out shortly afterwards, there were no incidents in Kilkee beyond the sending of a threatening letter to Dr Tuite. For this the secretary of the club, Patrick Kean Jr, was summoned before the magistrates and got away with a 'salutary stricture' for want of evidence.

In August Kilkee was visited by a group of military and police in search of some of the Young Ireland leaders whom they believed to be in hiding in the town. This was the outcome of a report that Richard O'Gorman and two companions had dined in one of the town's hotels on the previous day. At midnight the hotels and a number of private houses were surrounded and searched. 'The traitors were said to be disguised as females and occupied ladies' apartments; it therefore became absolutely necessary that all the ladies' bedrooms should be searched. This painful duty was performed by Mr Little RM alone and in the most delicate manner possible.' The search did not meet with any success. [The story of O'Gorman's escape to the United States is told in Ignatius Murphy's *The Diocese of Killaloe, 1800-1850*.]

Despite the troubled times, visitors still came to Kilkee in the summer of 1848. In the very early part of the season, in mid-June, the town was reported to be free from disease. But a month later fever in the surrounding countryside prevented visitors from making some of their usual excursions. One picnic party, which visited Dunlickey Castle, about four miles from the town along the coast, had an unusual experience, which illustrates the change brought about by famine. The party of visitors was held up by a group of about ten men with two or three guns, in what seemed to be an attempted robbery. However, the visitors, despite the presence of the guns, resisted their opponents and managed to put them to flight. Apart from the manner in which it ended, the incident was unusual in that it was the first occasion on which visitors to Kilkee were ever molested in this manner. Ten days later two men were charged at Kilkee Petty Sessions in connection with it. It now transpired that they were not attempting a robbery. The field in which the holiday party was enjoying itself belonged to one of the accused, and he claimed that he was merely trying to get money for the use of it, a claim which was accepted. The whole affair does, however, show the change which had taken place from pre-Famine times and how desperate some people had become.

Evictions

From the end of 1847 the lives of the people of Kilfearagh parish came to be dominated by three interconnected things – evictions, Kilrush Workhouse and emigration. In many cases evictions forced people to the workhouse, while some, in order to get aid from the workhouse, had to give up their plots of ground – so that their situation was very close to eviction.

We have already seen that, by the autumn of 1847, lack of money to pay rents and a desire for clearance because of rising rates had led to 6,000 notices to quit being served in Kilrush Union. Those who still had some money or stock were caught between the rival claims of rent and rate collectors. On 22 December Captain Mann remarked that the landlords were trying to extract their rents, while a few weeks earlier he had noted that some of the landlords, dissatisfied with their agents, had transferred their agencies to Marcus Keane, 'who is a well known stringent and successful collector or rents'. This was the same Marcus Keane who acted for Lord Conyngham in Kilfearagh parish and of whom the *Limerick Reporter* was to remark not very much later that he was 'unhappy when not exterminating'.

Captain Kennedy commented on the large sums being demanded as rent. An acre of land worth about 15s. was being let for £3, and the occupiers, being unable to pay, were bound to give 140 days' labour in spring and harvest-time when they needed it most themselves. Similarly, cabins worth about 7s. 6d. a year were being let for 100 or 120 days' labour.

As the stage was set for the mass evictions which were to follow, a tenant right meeting took place at Lisdeen, and a petition was adopted calling on the Government to extend the tenant right of Ulster to that locality. Captain Mann had been slightly worried before the meeting took place but after the event he could describe it as a 'very hole in the corner affair'. He must have been right, for nothing further was heard about tenant right from the area for quite some time.

When a landlord wished to evict, what did he do? The ordinary ejectment procedure involved getting the sheriff's authority and the serving of notices in advance to the people concerned including the local relief officer, 'to allow preparation to be made for the reception or subsistence of the families'. The majority of landlords in West Clare, however, found this a little too involved, and so they adopted different and simpler procedures. In most cases they moved by Civil Bill against the tenant for arrears of rent. He was then arrested and released only when possession had been given to the landlord by the other members of his family and he had agreed to having the house knocked down. Or, alternately, a small sum of money might be given to the tenant and a discharge from all claim of rent on his giving up possession and the house being demolished. However, when the Revd S. Godolphin Osborne visited West Clare in 1849, evictions witnessed by him involved the use of the first method. It is worth giving his account of this in full, as the scene described must have been typical of many:

> The legal forms necessary to obtain the Sheriff's authority to take possession having been gone through, and the proper notices served on the parties concerned, a notice is also served on the Relieving Officer, informing him on what day the people will be ejected. At the appointed hour we will suppose ourselves to be on the spot; there are, say, some six dwellings in a group, nearly adjoining each other, and all situated close to a public roadside. Some of these dwellings may be larger than others, but in outward form and actual structure they are all much alike, simply two stone gables, built of the stone of the country, a thatched roof connecting them, and descending to some five or six feet from the ground. A gig or outside car arrives with the Sheriff's deputy; the agent for the property is in attendance on horseback, with some ten or twelve rough looking peasants, one or two of them having iron crowbars and other necessaries for their business of destruction. A certain form is quickly gone through by the Law's Officer, the effect of which is, to put the Agent of the property in possession, in other words, giving him full power to turn out the people and pull down the dwellings, if it is his pleasure to do so. In very many districts a small body of armed police attend, in case of any forcible resistance. The Relieving Officer calls out the names from the list sent to him and, as he may think proper, offers to the parties now to be ejected orders for admission to the Union House. These orders are very generally refused, or if accepted, are not acted on.
>
> The word is now given by the Agent to his 'destructives'. If the people will not come out of the dwellings they are dragged out; with them the bed, kettle, old wheel, tub, and one or two stools, with perhaps an old chest; few cabins have anything to add to this list of furniture at the time the tenants are ejected; the living and dead stock being alike out in the road; now begins a long and long sustained chorus of intermingled prayers, blessings, reproaches, revilings, weeping, etc., generally ending in low monotonous imprecations on the heads of those who thus are crowning the ruin of the ejected.
>
> The women will 'kene', beat their breasts, throw themselves on the ground, embrace the knees of the Agent's horse, hang on to the steps of the Sheriff's car; they will do and say all an excited Irishwoman can say and do, to either obtain money, or invoke

vengeance; and truly poor creatures, they are gifted with powers of eloquence, aided by a power of action and gesticulation, which, as it may be employed, to bless or curse, is in either way most impressive.

Agents and sheriff's officers, however, from the nature of their avocation, have become case hardened against these attacks upon the softer feelings of our nature; the groans and prayers of the ejected, like the dust of the falling thatch of their roofs, are unavoidable evils, the regular result of the routine of 'house tumbling' ...

A man jumps up on the roof, and soon uncovers a part of the beam, which goes from the point of one gable to the other; he fastens a rope round it; it may require, perhaps, a little action from a saw, to weaken it; the rope is passed through the door of the house; it is manned at once by some others of the band; an iron bar is now placed under the wall plate, at one of the angles; a pull at the rope, breaking the back of the roof, and the lifting of the bar, hoisting it from its bearing on the wall, down it goes in a cloud of dust, sometimes falling wholly within the walls, sometimes a part will remain resting one end on the ground, the other against the gable.

The methods we have mentioned were within the law. But not all ejections followed exact legal procedures, and the poor tenant had little redress. One man, named Honan, from Tarmon, returned from a visit to Kilrush in search of outdoor relief to find that his cabin had been levelled in his absence. Knowing that this was illegal, he summoned the landlord to Kilrush Petty Sessions, won his case and was awarded £1 for the demolition of the cabin. But the landlord then appealed the sentence, knowing that Honan could not possibly afford the cost of this.

Between November 1847 and July 1848 about 900 houses, containing 4,000 inhabitants, were levelled in Kilrush Union, and still the work of destruction went on. In early March 1848, fifty-six people, many of whom had paid their rent, were evicted from their holdings at Emlagh near Kilkee. Their houses were levelled to the ground and their neighbours warned not to take them in. The remarks made by some of the evicted to a newspaper reporter must be expressive of the feelings of many such:

The landlords can transport or hang us – poverty is our only crime – many of us would pay our rent if left in – the landlords make a home-made Botany-bay of the Workhouse, but in New South Wales we would get enough to eat. Oh! the landlords don't want a Gallows-green while the Workhouse stands – that's what can clear their properties of the poor, who are ready to live by their work if they got it to do.

All through the summer and autumn the evictions went on. In October eighty-six people were evicted from O'Gorman Mahon property at Lisdeen, while fifty-five more were evicted by Colonel Vandeleur at Banemore. In November, 129 had to leave their homes at Lislanihan and 85 more at Termon. More evictions from O'Gorman Mahon property – 23 people this time. On condition of being allowed to take any of their crops they had to level their own houses. In mid-November the biggest eviction was from the Conyngham property at Kilfearagh – 107. These people had given up their lands in the previous May but were permitted to remain on in their homes as caretakers until the onset of winter, when they were eventually driven out and their houses levelled. In early December some 30-40 people were evicted in Kilkee. And so the numbers of homeless grew and grew. On 4 December 1848, Captain Kennedy stated that he had listed the eviction of 6,090 souls in Kilrush Union since the previous July. And the specific instances we have mentioned were probably just a few of the many in Kilfearagh parish.

After eviction the people just wandered about burrowing behind the ditches or under a few broken rafters of their old homes until eventually compelled to face towards the workhouse. Some got shelter from their neighbours, but when fever and dysentery made their appearance they were put out by the roadside to die. Some landlords, as we have already seen, forbade the neighbours to give shelter – because if the destitute remained in the locality they would have to be paid for by it in rates when they eventually went to the workhouse.

The final stage, then, was the workhouse. And Captain Kennedy has vividly described for us a typical scene while the evictions were in full swing. On 16 March 1848, he wrote:

> We admitted a considerable number of paupers, among whom were some of the most appalling cases of destitution and suffering it has ever been my lot to witness. The state of most of these wretched creatures is traceable to the numerous evictions which have lately taken place in the Union. When driven from their cabins they betake themselves to the ditches or the shelter of some bank and there exist like animals, till starvation or the inclemency of the weather drives them to the workhouse. There were three cartloads of these creatures, who could not walk, brought for admission yesterday, some in fever, some suffering from dysentery, and all from want of food. They were immediately handed over to the medical officer and provided with nourishment. I leave no effort untried to mitigate their misery.

It was Captain Kennedy who did most to alleviate in some little way the sufferings caused by the evictions in West Clare and soon afterwards to publicise them throughout Great Britain. Many years later, when he was staying with Lord Carnarvon at Highclere Castle, the conversation turned to the Irish Famine. A fellow guest has recorded Captain Kennedy's words to his host:

> I can tell you, my Lord, that there were days in that western county when I came back from some scene of eviction so maddened by the sights of hunger and misery I had seen in the day's work, that I felt disposed to take the gun from behind the door and shoot the first landlord I met.

A small incident which occurred at Kilkee in November-December 1848 is worth recalling. A poor man who had two goats supported himself by the sale of their milk. He fell into arrears with his rent, owing 10s. and for this his goats were seized by the bailiff. A benefactor, whom I think we can safely identify with Captain Kennedy, sent him the 10s. with which he could recover his goat – and later when the poor man was able to offer to return the money his benefactor refused it.

The lack of humanity and mercy displayed by landlord or agent in the above incident was terrifyingly common. In early 1848 some of the poor people realised that the Gregory clause could be circumvented by giving up the greater part of their land but retaining a little bit on which the cabin stood, less than a quarter acre. But Dr Foley of Kilrush cited the case of a poor widow who tried to keep her house. The landlord refused to accept the land without the house and as a result her claim for outdoor relief was objected to because she held more than a quarter acre. Dr Foley commented:

> Many landlords appear to be most anxious to take advantage of the present distressed and helpless conditions of the poor people holding one or more acres of land, and obliged for the present to seek the aid of legalised relief ...

The relaxation of the Gregory clause in May 1848, then, was a great boon to many poor people – provided they could pay the rent.

During 1848 and early 1849 Captain Kennedy's letters to the Poor Law Commissioners kept them informed in detailed fashion about the evictions in Kilrush Union. In April 1849 these letters were published in a Parliamentary Blue Book, and this brought the horror of the evictions before the British public. On 8 June Mr Poulett Scrope MP referred to them in the British House of Commons and Sir Robert Peel joined in the discussion, saying that he knew not if it were possible to apply a legislative remedy but he hoped that the expression of their abhorrence of such scenes might have some effect in checking them. This speech was greeted with cries of 'Hear, hear', which did little to check the work of destruction in Clare.

Meanwhile Marcus Keane was doing his utmost to discover inaccuracies in Captain Kennedy's reports, and in August he had a petition presented in the House of Commons embodying the results of his research. He could not, very obviously, deny the misery existing in the union, and so he had to adopt a different approach:

> These reports, your petitioner regrets to say, are not overdrawn, but he denies (so far as the properties under his management are concerned) that evictions, or the imposition of rackrents are at all the cause of the misery described.

It is doubtful if many believed that the rackrents and evictions were not making significant contribution to the misery.

The publication of the Blue Book brought Kilrush Union into the news in Britain for the first time, and it was to remain there for the next few years, as other reports came in on the happenings in the West of Clare. In the autumn of 1849 Poulett Scrope, who had already shown concern at the evictions, travelled over to make a personal investigation. He saw for himself that the reports were by no means exaggerated, and he calculated that 20,000 had been evicted in Kilrush Union in the previous two years. And where were these at the time of his visit? In his own words: 'My informants assured me that, to the best of their knowledge, the greater number of these are dead.'

Another visitor in mid-1849 was the Hon. and Revd S. Godolphin Osborne, who incorporated the results of his observations in Clare and elsewhere into his book, *Gleanings in the West of Ireland*. Of the evictions in Kilrush Union he said that, although Captain Kennedy's reports had often been declared to be exaggerations, in his view no report could exaggerate the amount of wholesale house levelling which had taken place. And at the end of the year a reporter from the *Illustrated London News* toured the union. His reports and accompanying sketches bore out everything that had already been said. To him the unroofed walls which had been left standing in many instances were like 'the tombs of a departed race'. 'I felt actually relieved at seeing one or two half-clad spectres gliding about, as an evidence that I was not in the land of the dead.'

The visitors to Kilkee in the summer of 1849 must also have been keenly aware of the great misery and distress in the countryside, because when travelling on picnics and excursions they were surrounded on all sides by grim evidence of the mass evictions. One person's jarvey gave a brief but penetrating reminder, when, pointing at one of the ruined cabins, he merely remarked: 'There's more of it, sir.' Then, immediately changing the tone of his voice, he continued: 'Isn't it a rale fine day and isn't that as good driving as ever you had in them nasty steam coaches that's breaking all the poor boys wid horses ...'

Despite fears of competition the jarveys were not too badly off – much better off than most others, as they still had a source of income. As we have seen, the evicted in their destitution finally faced the workhouse in Kilrush and they were accompanied in their journey by others who were not yet homeless but had absolutely no resources left. In the next chapter we will attempt to trace the history of the workhouse in these years, catering as it did for thousands of people from Kilfearagh among many others. The fortunes of the workhouse were the fortunes of a large proportion of the population of Kilfearagh.

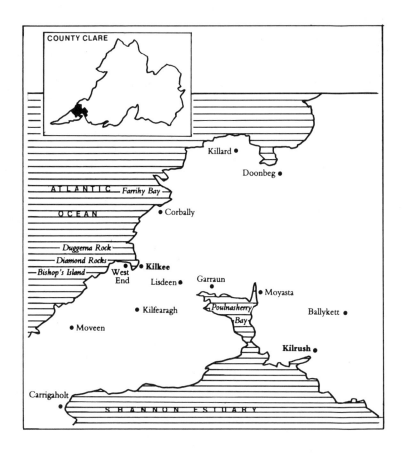

West Clare, particularly Kilfearagh parish

Kilrush Workhouse

ARRIVAL OF CAPTAIN KENNEDY

In November 1847, with the beginning of the mass evictions in the union, Kilrush Workhouse came under heavy pressure for the first time and was ill equipped to meet the demands made upon it. However, this was not altogether surprising, as these demands went far beyond anything ever envisaged. It was at this stage that Captain Kennedy arrived on the scene as Poor Law Inspector, and he, more than anybody else, tried to get the workhouse resources organised to meet the crisis. Indeed, it can be said that but for his work during the next two and a half years a very great tragedy would have been far worse. And this was not merely a matter of organisation on his part. As time went on, he had also to face intense opposition from the better-off classes because of his exposure of the evictions and his attempts to secure an adequate poor law rate.

When Captain Kennedy arrived in Kilrush in early November 1847, he found that the running of the workhouse was being performed in a far from efficient manner. In a letter to the Poor Law Commissioners he wrote:

> I need not recapitulate the numerous and culpable irregularities I have found to exist in the house, and which I have undertaken to correct by daily visits. How the house has so long escaped general infection I am at a loss to conceive. On the last visiting day I found a side gate open, and free access for the friends of fever patients to pass to and from the hospital.

Immediately he began to make arrangements to have the fever patients removed to other premises, but a full month slipped by before he succeeded in doing so.

The school for the children in the workhouse he described as 'a mere farce'. 'The master utterly unfit for that or any other calling; attending his school is a pure waste of time.' The master of the workhouse itself he described as 'inert and ... too old to learn those habits of order and regularity necessary to the Government and well being of a large Body.' And soon afterwards he wrote: 'The house has improved in order and cleanliness, but I apprehend no permanent improvement can result under the present master.' The assistant master and matron, however, he regarded as zealous and efficient. In late December the Poor Law Commissioners issued an order removing the master from his office.

Before Captain Kennedy's arrival, the capacity of the workhouse had already been increased from its original 800 to 1,100. And in the following two years a number of additional buildings were taken over, so that eventually the original workhouse and its six auxiliaries were capable of accommodating over 5,000 people. However, in November 1847 it could as yet take only about 1,100, and by the middle of the month – because of the numerous evictions – the house was crowded with more and more clamouring for admission. One day alone nearly two hundred people were taken in. Captain Kennedy wrote:

> Such a tangled mass of poverty, filth and disease, as the applicants presented, I have never seen. Numbers in all stages of fever and small-pox mingling indiscriminately with the crowd, and all clamouring for admission. I had them separated as quickly as possible ... it was really an appalling sight.

But before very long he was to grow accustomed to even more terrible scenes.

DEMAND FOR OUTDOOR RELIEF

In mid November no outdoor relief had as yet been given to anybody. But, as pressure on the workhouse increased, it was decided to grant it to the non-able-bodied destitute in order that these people could leave the workhouse and make room for the ablebodied. The outdoor relief was to consist of food alone, despite a recommendation from Captain Kennedy, with the backing of the Poor Law Commissioners, to give cash as well. Two and a half years later, in a report drawn up for Parliament, Poulett Scrope commented on the results of this policy:

> The outdoor relief afforded ... has been always limited to a weekly dole of raw meal alone, clearly inadequate, under the circumstances of the great bulk of the recipients, to preserve them from gradual decay if not immediate starvation, through want of the other ordinary necessaries of life.

With a promise, then, of supplies of food but of nothing else, many of the poor women and children went out of the workhouse – not always with good results. On 14 December Captain Mann wrote:

> A man and his family who were in the house and whose case left no doubt as to their utter destitution were removed out of it on out relief,

in order to make room for receiving able-bodied claimants in. The change from the comfort inside the House to what they could get out, had the effect of causing the poor children to get ill, and three died in ten days.

To the able-bodied there was to be no relief except in the workhouse. And for a while in December there was such a clamour for admission that, as Mann remarked, the workhouse would have been swamped if the Gregory clause had not been strictly enforced. Others tried to bring pressure on the authorities to give outdoor relief to the able-bodied. When Captain Kennedy arrived at the workhouse on 1 December, he was faced with what seems to have been an organised demonstration. Although it was still morning, a crowd of about 1,000 had already assembled near the workhouse. Soon a general cry for outdoor relief was begun, accompanied by a waving of blackthorn sticks. Captain Kennedy then addressed the crowd, some of whom made an unsuccessful attempt to force the outer gate of the workhouse. One who struck Captain Kennedy was dragged in and placed in the lockup, and shortly afterwards he was joined by eight or nine others. This quietened the crowd. Meanwhile, a continuous stream of people was seen approaching from the Kilkee direction. Colonel Vandeleur, Chairman of the Board of Guardians, had been on his way to Kilkee, but when he met the large crowds he considered it more prudent to turn back. Before long the crowd outside the workhouse, augmented by the new arrivals from Kilkee, had swelled to about 3,000. The police and a troop of military were the next to arrive on the scene. Fortunately, prudence prevailed at this stage and the people dispersed, leaving the really destitute to apply for admission to the workhouse. Subsequently three hundred of these were taken in.

In his report to the Poor Law Commissioners on 2 December, Captain Kennedy pointed out that this had been an organised demonstration, engineered, it would seem, by Fr Comyn:

> A more bare faced attempt at intimidation I have never seen – Four fifths of this mob were from 'Kilkee' and a part of 'Moyarta' district – and it is with pain I am constrained to believe they were *encouraged* and *incited* to this *turbulent demonstration* by their Roman Catholic pastor with a view to compel the Guardians to give indiscriminate 'outdoor relief'. This Reverend Gentleman's conduct is I fear generally an exception to that of his Brother Clergymen in this Union – who seek to mitigate suffering and support the law.

On 31 December the Poor Law Commissioners authorised outdoor relief for the able-bodied, while laying down certain conditions.

1. That the relief, which could be given in food alone, should, as far as practicable, be in cooked food.

2. That every able-bodied male relieved should, as far as practicable, be set to perform a task of work during eight hours at least of every day for which he received relief.

3. That no able-bodied person in employment, nor any part of his family, should receive relief under the order.

Although the Guardians now had authorisation to give outdoor relief to the able-bodied, they were quite reluctant to do so, and Captain Kennedy concurred with them in this. Despite threats, as when Colonel Vandeleur and Kennedy were warned to have their wills made, this course of action was persevered in for about three months – probably until mid-April, when there was a sudden big jump in the numbers relieved. The long deferment of the relief was partly explained by Captain Kennedy when he wrote: 'The lamentable want of truth and shame would render it a matter of great difficulty to distinguish between the really destitute and the shameless beggar.' There was also a further factor. In January and February, for reasons which we shall see, there was an extreme reluctance to enter the workhouse, and while there were places available in the house it was official policy not to give outdoor relief. Otherwise, as Captain Mann remarked: 'One general ruin would be the result,' because nobody would want to enter the house and the finance of the union would probably break under the strain of having to feed huge numbers outside.

THE 'SLAUGHTER HOUSE'

On Captain Kennedy's arrival, as we have seen, he immediately tried to make provision to get the fever patients removed from the workhouse to separate premises. He met with some difficulty in procuring a building for the purpose and eventually had to make do with the slaughter house of a bacon store. His purpose in making the new arrangement was to prevent the spread of infection. But, in fact, after the new premises had been occupied the situation worsened and the number of deaths began to go up. In the last week of the old year 60 of the 131 patients in the temporary fever hospital died. On one morning, when Captain Kennedy visited it, he found that eight patients had died in the previous night. Two relieving officers, the matron and assistant master of the workhouse were themselves down with fever, while the nurses and attendants in the fever hospital were so scared that it was only with difficulty that they could be prevailed upon to perform their duties.

In the first week of the new year seventy-five people died in the fever hospital, about thirty-five per cent of the weekly admissions. Captain Mann was convinced that this was not due to neglect but was caused by the fact that most of those admitted were nearly dead already in any case. However, this was not seen by people considering entrance to the workhouse. Finally, one particular case dispelled any remaining doubts. A car brought four people in from the country. When taken from the cart at the workhouse, two were found to be already dead; one died during the night and the fourth next day. When the report got into circulation that the four had died within a day of arriving at the workhouse, the general view was confirmed that it was certain death to go into it. And the fever hospital came to be known once again as the Slaughter House, though this time in a different context from previously. The overall result was an extreme reluctance to enter the workhouse, so that, even though thousands of people were starving most of them remained outside. And as long as there were vacant places in the house, outdoor relief would not be given to the able-bodied.

Previously most people had been very reluctant to enter. Mr C.W. Hamilton had commented in early 1846 that it was too much to expect that a labourer who had been hitherto independent 'should at once yield and with his whole family (for they must all go) leave his house ... passing at once from a position of honourable independence to that which he looks upon as the lowest state of degradation'. This aversion was now strengthened with an even more compelling motive for remaining outside so that many only came to the workhouse as a very last resort. On Dr Madden's visit to Kilrush in early 1851 he found that this was the case with the applicants for admission with whom he spoke:

> These applicants for admission into the Kilrush Poorhouse ... had only come there when every other means of sustaining life had failed. There was not one of those I questioned who had not a mortal terror of that Poorhouse of Kilrush, and had not overcome it, only when the charity on which they had eked out a miserable existence had been utterly exhausted, or when the use of the boiled nettles and other weeds which had been their food of late had brought them to the brink of the grave.

DISMISSAL OF GUARDIANS

By mid-February Captain Kennedy was complaining of the inefficiency of the Kilrush Board of Guardians, and a week later he wrote: 'I have no confidence in the energy or foresight of the Board of Guardians as a body should serious difficulties arise.' A number of factors forced him to this conclusion ... One was the election, with only two dissentient votes, of Mr Pat Kelly (son of the previous master) as master. Captain Kennedy described him as 'a mere lad and in my opinion (as that of the Chairman of the Board) utterly incompetent for such a charge'. But the matter which finally brought affairs to a head was a financial crisis which struck the union at the end of February. On the 24th of the month the treasurer had a mere £50 in hands while debts amounted to nearly £1,000. Captain Mann, who was supplying the rye meal required to give outdoor relief to 10,000 people, was owed £120 and refused to give further supplies until paid. Colonel Vandeleur was absent, probably recuperating from a severe illness which he had suffered in January, and Captain Kennedy was quite certain that in his absence the Guardians would not be able to obtain any credit as they had the confidence of neither the public nor of the bankers.

However, there was one apparent temporary solution to the problem. Captain Mann had some funds given to him by the British Association, and Captain Kennedy now applied to him for a loan in order to be able to keep up the outdoor relief during the following week. Captain Mann felt that, in the circumstances, he had no option but to oblige. But he was also quick to point out that the reason for the crisis was the non-payment of rates by many, and these included quite a number of the *ex officio* and elected Guardians. Among the defaulters there were also some magistrates 'who have signed distress warrants for rates on poor wretches who have perhaps but a house or cow to support them'.

When Trevelyan heard what had happened, he could scarcely believe it. If it was true that the funds of the British Association had been used to make good the default of magistrates and Guardians, then, in his view, it was a great abuse and would have to be remedied by an effective collection of rates. And within a week the Poor Law Commissioners had made an order dissolving the Kilrush Board of Guardians. They were to be replaced by two paid Vice-Guardians. This step, however, was by no means unusual. Within the previous twelve months, half of the Boards of Guardians in Ireland had been dissolved, mainly because they had been unwilling to collect sufficient rates. In Kilrush also the chief reason was a financial one. In the previous August an average rate of 4s. 11d. in the £, amounting to £8,884, had been struck. By the end of January £4,948 of this had been used, leaving a balance of £3,936 to be collected to meet liabilities until the following July. Clearly this sum was going to be inadequate, and on 29 January Colonel Vandeleur made this point in a letter to Sir R. Routh: 'It is perfectly clear the Union will not be able to meet the demands upon it without assistance from Government.' Such demands for assistance were the last thing the Government wished to hear of and so, when the financial crisis came in late February and early March, the dissolution of the Board of Guardians was almost inevitable.

The Guardians' point, in not wishing to strike a new rate before July, was that 4s. 11d. was the most that could be demanded during the course of a year. They probably had selfish motives in asserting this, but there was also the valid point that the impoverished union could not afford even this rate and that the collection of it was bringing some ratepayers themselves down to destitution level. Six months later this point was acknowledged at government level when Twisleton told Trevelyan that it would be unwise to insist on a larger rate than 5s. 'I believe,' he wrote, ' that more money is likely to be realised with a 5s. rate than with a rate of a larger amount.'

The new Vice-Guardians in Kilrush Union appear to have got over the financial crisis by means of borrowing and assiduously collecting the remainder of the current rate. A new rate was not stuck until August. In Kilkee Electoral Division it was expected that the rate would be fifty per cent higher than in the previous year, when it was the highest in the country – six in ten. However, Captain Kennedy used some money obtained from the British Association to subsidise the poor rate, and as a result it was only 3s. As a mark of their gratitude to Captain Kennedy, the people of Kilkee lit large bonfires and carried a lighted tar barrel around on men's shoulders.

About the same time as the dismissal of the Guardians there was another minor crisis at Kilrush Workhouse. When the fever mortality was very high in early January, Captain Kennedy sent a special report on the matter to the Poor Law Commissioners, and the result of this was an inspection by Dr Phelan, who ordered changes in diet and medical treatment. One of the workhouse doctors, Dr Donovan, did not take too kindly to this and shortly afterwards he resigned, although the Guardians had passed a vote of 'unbounded confidence' in their two doctors.

FURTHER DOWNHILL

As 1848 progressed it was clear that the whole situation was still getting worse rather than better. In 1847 only a small acreage had been planted with potatoes. In 1848 with renewed hope the people made very great sacrifices to plant as much as possible, and this was as true of West Clare as elsewhere. In Clare as a whole, 16,836 acres were planted with potatoes compared with 6,129 in 1847. The acreage planted with beans also rose from 642 acres to 1,411, while the turnip acreage fell from 10,988 to 8,032. But the expectations were, unfortunately, not fulfilled. In the latter part of July symptoms of the blight were noticed at Kilkee, though it did not appear to be nearly as bad as in '46 and '47. However, as time passed the situation worsened. On 25 August *The Times* of London printed a letter from Kilkee which stated that the late potatoes on the west coast were gone and that the early ones were going. Potatoes, beans and turnips were being plundered nightly. The writer concluded on a very pessimistic note: 'Altogether the prospects here are far more awful this winter than at any of the worst periods these three years.' And ten days previously Twisleton had written to Trevelyan in a similar vein but with more general application: 'We have another visitation of the potato disease this year ... The empire will reel under this blow.'

Two months later the *Limerick Chronicle* commented on the Kilkee area: 'Plundering is worse this season than last year. Neither gardens, haggards or houses escape.' And the reason for this can be readily seen in one of Captain Kennedy's reports:

> During my attendance at the admission on two days and part of a third, I took the opportunity of inquiring of every able-bodied applicant where and with whom he had last been employed and at what rate of wages? Almost the whole number declared that even during the harvest, they had laboured for 2*d.* and 3*d.* per day, seldom getting 4*d.*, and that at present they could not exchange or obtain their food for their labour ... I believe (however incredible it may appear) that nineteen-twentieths of the labouring population of the Kilrush Union are without employment or resource of any kind, nor do I see any attempt to remedy this state of things, though the land is undrained and not half cultivated.

And during all this time the evictions were continuing.

As the new year approached, another shadow appeared on the horizon. In December 1848 an outbreak of Asiatic cholera, or the 'devouring pestilence', as the *Clare Journal* described it, made its appearance in Belfast. From there it spread throughout the country, reaching its peak in May, but declining in most parts in June. As the epidemic was gaining in force, the Central Board of Health in Dublin sent out many circulars with instructions for setting up special dispensaries, nursing etc. However, all expenses had to be met out of Union funds. In March 1849 the cholera made its appearance in West Clare and a cholera hospital was established at Kilkee. Among the people there was near panic, though the outbreak of the disease in the area does not appear to have been very severe. Captain Kennedy remarked that the temporary hospitals at Kilkee and Carrigaholt were made necessary not so much by the cholera itself as by 'choleraphobia'. And he continued: 'Such is the senseless dread of this disease that any wretched creature afflicted with diarrhoea is immediately supposed to be a cholera case and thrown out of their lodging.' In early April, accompanied by Dr O'Donnell, he visited the cholera hospitals at Kilkee and Carrigaholt in an attempt 'to allay popular excitement'.

By the end of April Dr Griffin, the local medical officer, was able to give a good report of the cholera situation in Kilkee. His letter also gives some indications of the procedures adopted to combat the spread of the disease:

> A few cases of the disease did occur here, the first being persons who came ill from Limerick, but owing to the speedy removal of those

attacked, the cleansing, whitewashing the houses of the poor, and other measures promptly adopted by the local Sanatory [*sic*] Committee, the further spread of the malady has been effectually checked; and I am happy to state that no case has occurred in the village or the immediate neighbourhood for several days past. I may also add, that the mortality amongst those attacked has been very much below the average.

The summer season in Kilkee in 1849 was not very much affected by the cholera or by the plight of the rural population. At the end of July the town was full, with scarcely a lodge vacant, and this situation lasted until well on into September. There were the usual dances in the lodges, races on the strand and in mid-August a three-day regatta was held. However, though outward appearances were maintained and the round of entertainment was very much as in pre-Famine times, visitors to Kilkee during this summer could not but be aware of the dreadful condition of most of the natives of West Clare. A visitor wrote in mid August: 'Embarrassment, distress and misery are experienced in Kilkee, exorbitant as the prices are at which some of the lodges are temporarily let.' And of the immediate countryside another visitor reported in September that there were no cattle at all left and that few of the ratepayers had either a cow, a sheep or a horse. All were being reduced to the one common denominator. In mid September three fishermen were drowned at Farrihy while trying to snatch a meagre living from the sea. Others had to give up the attempt as they were too weak to row and just 'died away'.

In October the Earl of Arundel and Surrey visited Kilrush and Kilkee to view the situation at first hand. Accompanied by William Monsell and Aubrey de Vere, he inspected Kilrush Workhouse and was favourably impressed by the arrangements there. Of their visit to Kilkee, Aubrey de Vere wrote in his *Recollections*:

> We passed the next day in roaming over famine-stricken moors and bogs in the neighbourhood, then among the most severely tried districts of Ireland. I shall not soon forget one visit, which, accompanied by the local inspector, we paid to a deserted cabin among the morasses. Its only inmate was a little infant, whose mother was most likely seeking milk for it. On slightly moving the tattered coverlet of the cradle, a shiver ran over the whole body of the infant and the next moment the dark emaciated little face relapsed into stillness. Probably the mother returned to find her child dead. Mr Monsell burst into a flood of tears. Nothing was said; but a few days later, on Lord Arundel's return to England, the inspector at Kilkee received a letter from him enclosing a cheque for £200 to be added to the local famine fund.

To the *Clare Journal* Kilkee was now the *Deserted Village*, and in November its Kilkee correspondent reported that within a few miles of the town the tenants had left their farms, carrying with them all their movable possessions if they had not already converted them into money. 'High rents, no abatements, low prices for agricultural produce have discouraged them.' This was one of the first indications of the vast emigration movement which was now in its initial stages in West Clare, and of which we shall see more later. And it was at this stage that another and far more serious financial crisis hit Kilrush Union.

FINANCIAL CRISIS

In the spring of 1849 the Government came forward with a new plan to give financial assistance to the poorer unions – a plan which would involve very little expense to itself. A rate-in-aid was to be levied on the more prosperous unions, and, in addition, a rate of 6d. in the £ was to be paid by every union, against which the Treasury would make advances, not exceeding £100,000, for relief. As a result of this, Kilrush Union benefited to the extent of £15,000 between March and November 1849. Yet, despite this assistance, when the time came to strike a new rate for the union in November, its liabilities were £15,000, liabilities which could be only partially balanced by £4,500 in rates which were still outstanding.

It was against this background that the paid Vice-Guardians, who had been in charge of the union for the previous eighteen months, were replaced by a new Board of Guardians on 27 October. The first and most pressing duty of the members of the Board was to strike a new rate, and this they did on 10 November. To meet all the demands being made upon them by their own unaided resources, they would have had to strike a rate varying from 19s. 11½d. in Kilrush electoral district to 41s. 3½d. for Killard. The Kilkee rate would have been 33s. 5½d. It would have been sheer madness to do this, and so, quite rightly, they decided that there was no point in attempting the impossible. However, they probably set their sights too low when they settled on a flat rate of 3s. for the union. At their next meeting, on the 17th, Mr Lynch, a Poor Law Inspector, told them that the rate they had struck would realise only £7,000, whereas £36,000 was needed. And, addressing a group many of whom had landed interests, he continued: 'It is not the rates but the rents that are ruining your country.' But there can be no doubt that there was much to be said for the action of the Guardians. Fifteen months previously, Twisleton had remarked on the futility of striking a rate above 5s. – and the situation was now immeasurably worse.

At the meeting Captain Kennedy drew attention to the Guardians' imme- diate problem – how and where, without money, they were to obtain supplies for the ensuing week. This crisis was somehow overcome, but it was to recur week after week while the union finances remained in a precarious state. On 24 November the Guardians were informed by the Poor Law Commissioners of the inadequacy of the rate they had struck and that one of from 11s. to 21s. was needed. Captain Kennedy also pointed out that they could not expect any help from the Treasury unless they agreed on a reasonable rate. The Guardians now decided to raise the rate – but it was a mere gesture – from 3s. to 3s. 6d., declaring, with a good deal of truth, that a higher rate could never be collected. They also decided to effect some economies and, on a split vote, withdrew the outdoor temporary medical department of the union, that is, medical attendance at some places distant from the workhouse. The rate, small as it was, had not yet been collected. Owing to the already huge debt it was impossible to get supplies until eventually a few of the Guardians personally went security. In this way 13,000 people were tided over the last few days of November.

In early December the breaking point was finally reached. A reporter who visited the workhouse found that there was not even sufficient food to give the inmates their dinner:

> The Master and the Matron, fearing the worst, exerted themselves in the early hours of the day, and had a quantity of turnips and parsnips which were grown in the workhouse ground boiled; and on this species of food the paupers dined.

For five days these vegetables remained the chief food in the workhouse. During this period 600-700 people who arrived from Kilmurry, Killofin and Kilkee seeking admission were sent home again as they could not be fed.

The Board of Guardians now decided that the only remedy was to appeal to the Poor Law Commissioners for help, and a memorial outlining their case was despatched:

> Resolved, that having been refused further supplies by Mr Russell and other merchants, or any advance of money by our treasurer, we call the attention of the Commissioners to the awful state of the Union, with 12,000 on the outdoor relief, without rations for the current week, with over 2,000 inmates in the workhouse and auxiliaries, and no provision for their next meal, except turnips, which has been their principal food for the last two days, and we feel satisfied that unless immediate assistance be sent us, the consequence will be fearful in the extreme.

But the Commissioners were not inclined to listen very sympathetically to this request, as they felt that the Guardians could get money from rates. And as the wrangle continued, the people starved owing to the stoppage of outdoor relief.

In this situation crowds from the outlying parishes began to throng to Kilrush in the hope of getting something to eat. On 12 December the *Limerick and Clare Examiner* carried a report from a Kilrush correspondent:

> The streets of our town are thronged – shopdoors choked up ... with swarms of famished miserable beings, piteously screaming and craving the least morsel of food. Along the roads that lead to the town may be seen numbers of cars laden with emaciated, half-naked creatures, huddled together in loathsome squalidness, proceeding towards the workhouse, where they hope to be relieved; but whence, alas! after they remain shivering and fainting whole days, and some times nights together, they are obliged to return to their hovels to die in despair, or, if they prefer it, to rush upon the town like wild and raving maniacs.

On the evening of 12 December about forty people boarded a ferry which would take them across the mouth of Poulnasherry Bay and so shorten their journey to the West – after most of them had spent a fruitless day waiting for food in Kilrush. About halfway across the boat sank and all were drowned except about three. Some of those whose bodies were washed ashore on the following morning were interred in the little burial ground at Kilnagalliagh. It was little wonder that a local poet was prompted to write of the hardships in Kilrush Union in 1849:

> Without a prayer or passing bell,
> The shroudless armies hourly swell.
> Miserere!
> The dying, ghastlier than the dead;
> With blanched lips have vainly said,
> 'Give us this day our daily bread.'
> Parce nobis Domine!

A day or two after the ferry disaster, Colonel Vandeleur and others of the Guardians were pelted with mud and missiles and hooted at their every appearance in public by those who had been refused outdoor relief. And the *Limerick Reporter* stated:

> The town (of Kilrush) is in danger, and guarded by policemen, who move constantly through the streets. The excitement is immense.

For nearly eight weeks outdoor relief remained suspended. On 27 December Captain Kennedy wrote: 'No kind of property is safe out of doors; but to say the truth there is little to steal beyond a few miserable cattle, which are housed at night.' And he added: 'Those who are absolutely in want are without the strength or energy to commit a robbery.' During this period those who survived had nothing to eat but a few turnips, given in charity by farmers who now had very little left themselves. And on the sea-coast there was a plentiful supply of shellfish.

Yet, even at the height of this crisis, as Christmas approached, a number began to leave the workhouse. This was a regular occurrence during the famine years. Many left the workhouse for the festival but returned again during the following week. For, despite all the want and suffering, Christmas was still the season of goodwill. 'Charity is liberally given, and hordes of both stationary and strolling poor subsist on it during the Christmas holidays.'

In the workhouse itself, because of the food crisis, Christmas seems to have been even grimmer than usual. A reporter wrote:

> The Guardians carefully and considerately guarded the poor in this workhouse from the invidious approach of appoplexy [sic], by a water gruel diet; and practically persuaded the outdoor poor that they were keeping Lent instead of Christmas, by a total deprivation of any kind of food.

As the New Year dawned the crisis continued. A letter to the *Limerick and Clare Examiner* from Kilrush expressed the despair, hopelessness and anger felt by many:

> Every day brings a fresh bundle to the faggot heap by which the funeral pyre of the old Celtic race is burned to cinders. Landlords crippled – farmers crushed – shopholders ruined – and the poor rotting in heaps – aye, in heaps, among the bogs and ditch-pits of the country.

When a reporter of the *Clare Journal* visited Lisdeen, he found its people very badly off. The village was part of the estate of the O'Gorman Mahon but had passed into the hands of a receiver who, for some time previously, had been carrying out the functions of a landlord. And around the village were cabins of people who had been evicted elsewhere and had congregated here. Their lifeline had been the outdoor relief until its suspension.

Meanwhile, attention remained focussed on the workhouse and Guardians. The latter, having received bad publicity since their reconstitution, excluded newspaper reporters from their meetings. Their chairman, Colonel Vandeleur, in a letter to the Poor Law Commissioners, argued that a higher rate would 'render the district a waste', and he attributed a good deal of the existing troubles to the facility with which outdoor relief had been given. As a result of it, he said, the people had lost all dependence on their own exertions. It was clear that, if he could help it, outdoor relief would be given as seldom and to as few as possible in the future. About the same time it was rumoured that steps were being taken against Captain Kennedy who was somewhat of an embarrassment. And when Vandeleur went to Dublin, probably to press home his case with the Poor Law Commissioners, people saw his journey as an attempt to get rid of Kennedy.

Eventually outdoor relief was restored. Then, after a short period, it was cut off again, possibly because the contractors were pressing for payment of their debts. The money collected under the rate struck in November was all but exhausted, and the only remedy was to strike a supplementary rate. Meanwhile, many charitable persons tried to help out in at least a little way by sending contributions to the parish priest of Kilrush, Fr Kenny. Some of this money he placed at the disposal of the local St Vincent de Paul Society, more of it he gave to the parish priests of the neighbouring parishes, probably including Kilfearagh, to meet cases of extreme necessity. And all the time, the poor of Kilfearagh, Moyarta and other western parishes kept pouring into Kilrush in the hope of faring better there than at home. Fr Kenny wrote: 'The houses of the benevolent and good are actually assailed by destitute persons supplicating relief. Their lamentations and shrieks are truly heart-rending.' In early February the St Vincent de Paul Society gathered a crowd of these poor people into a large timber-yard and distributed one penny each to 3,102 persons. Yet, during this period, Kilrush port was exporting corn in fairly large quantities.

At the end of March the Kilrush Guardians petitioned Parliament for help, a petition which drew from *The Times* the rejoinder that in that area all alike, proprietors, paupers, priests, etc., were joined in a conspiracy 'to deceive the state, to defraud one another, to evade the laws and pervert relief'. In Kilkee there was very definitely an attempt to defraud the Guardians when a number of the wealthier lodge-owners, who were non-resident for the greater part of the year, claimed that they should have to pay less in rates on the ground that they were not in occupation when the rate was struck. But the Poor Law Commissioners, when consulted, stated that the occupation of houses during the bathing season should be held as equivalent to occupation throughout the entire year. From a letter to the *Limerick and Clare Examiner* it would appear that towards the end of 1849 these same wealthy lodge-owners had petitioned the Poor Law Commissioners that the West End of Kilkee should be joined to a different electoral district in which the rates would be lower – as they felt that they should not have to contribute to the maintenance of the numerous paupers who had settled in the less fashionable part of the town.

Despite everything, Kilrush Union managed to weather the storm in the early part of 1850, and the Government was soon again giving grants from the rate in aid. However, on at least one occasion the workhouse must have been on the verge of closure and, of course, the outdoor relief was suspended for long periods.

IN KILRUSH WORKHOUSE

We have already seen that Colonel Vandeleur was not very much in favour of outdoor relief. The alternative was to increase the numbers of workhouse inmates, and these climbed very rapidly from the beginning of January 1850 onwards. By early June there were almost 5,000 people in Kilrush Workhouse and its auxiliaries, practically double the amount at the beginning of the year. No doubt, too, the Guardians' policy was aided by the uncertainty of outdoor relief, which was cut off several times in late winter and spring. And Kilfearagh parish provided its own proportion of these – on 31 January alone it was reported that there were 250 applicants for admission from Kilkee. In fact, most admission days saw huge crowds from all parts clamouring to get in, and the procedure adopted meant that many of them might have to go away unheard. Every applicant had to have his case for admission examined by some of the Guardians, and if there were not enough of them present many might have to go away without even getting an opportunity of making an application – and they would have to wait until the next admission day, a week later. Captain Kennedy, in one of his reports, described the situation on 2 February:

> The list was not commenced till 3 p.m. and the more distant divisions, Kilballyowen and Kilmurry, were not commenced till 6 p.m. when the majority of applicants, having fifteen or twenty miles to travel, had returned home and did not appear. The applicants from Kildysart, Kilfiddane and Kilkee were sent away undecided on.

And three months later the same thing was still happening. Although at least three Guardians were present on 9 May, the chairman alone was ruling the books and 'thirty-six hours would certainly not have sufficed to hear and rule each case'. As a result, many again had to be sent away unheard and unrelieved. Captain Kennedy's comment was: 'I think that this system is carried on to an unwarrantable and impolitic extent.' One suspects that it was used as a method of controlling numbers when there were too many applications.

What was life like in the workhouse for the many people from Kilfearagh parish who entered it at this period? On 25 March 1850 the diet provided for the inmates was as follows:

1. Able-bodied Working Males
Breakfast – 6 oz. Indian Meal; 2 oz. rice; 1 oz. butter
Dinner – 16 oz. rye and whole flour bread; 2 pints soup.

2. Able-bodied Working Females
Breakfast – 5½oz. Indian Meal and 1½ oz. rice; 1 oz. butter
Dinner – 14 oz. rye and whole flour bread; 1½ pints soup.

3. Persons not at work, and Infirm
Breakfast – 4½ oz. Indian meal and 1½ oz. rice; 1 oz. butter
Dinner – 12 oz. rye and whole flour bread; 1½ oz. soup

4. Children under 15 and over 9
Breakfast – 3¾ oz. Indian meal; 1¼ oz. rice; ½ pint new milk
Dinner – 10 oz. rye and whole flour bread; 1 pint soup
Supper – 4 oz. rye and whole flour bread; ½ pint soup.

This was the official diet, giving two meals a day to adults. But when a financial crisis struck, the paupers could find themselves dining mainly on turnips, as in December, or on half rations, as happened in late February.

The average cost of the food per inmate at this period was probably scarcely a penny a day. At any rate, a year later when the diet had improved to some extent, it was costing only 8*d.* per week per person. Dr Madden commented on it at this stage: 'In the Kilrush dietary, then, we look in vain for animal food, for vegetables, for milk and indeed for bread fit for the food of man.'

As the numbers admitted to the workhouse grew, so also did the numbers requiring treatment in the infirmary. A visitor in April 1850 said he found four boys and one man, all of them ill, in a bed not too large for one person. Colonel Vandeleur's reply was that they had two beds drawn together. A year later, commenting on a remark that there were three patients in each bed in the infirmary, he said that there were 79 beds for 180 patients 'so that few of the beds contained three patients'. Seemingly he regarded this as quite satisfactory. Throughout the remainder of the workhouse it is doubtful if the situation was any better.

Another complaint made about the house, and quite a serious one, was the want of sufficient warmth during the winter of 1849-50. And even for a while, though it was surrounded by bogs, there was a total lack of fires. At first sight, poor heating might not seem to be a very serious complaint. But the people of West Clare always had a very abundant supply of turf and were used to well-heated even if smoky houses. Captain Kennedy remarked that they complained more of the want of sufficient warmth than of any other part of the discipline of the workhouse. He also hinted rather broadly that something could be done about this. Colonel Vandeleur, however, felt that it would be impossible to give satisfaction with large numbers, as in their own homes they had been accustomed 'to sit in very large chimneys'.

MORTALITY

As the Guardians and Captain Kennedy grappled with vast financial and organisational problems in the early months of 1850, memories of the Slaughter House revived once again with a rapidly rising death rate. There had been 505 deaths in the workhouse in the year ended 29 September 1849 – a big decrease from the 1,070 in 1847 and perhaps reflecting the improvements brought about by Captain Kennedy. But the tide had turned again with a vengeance, and in the month of April 1850 alone 213 deaths occurred. And in the twelve months from 25 March 1850 to 25 March 1851 the total number of deaths was about 1,700 or an average of 140 per month. Mr W.H. Lucas, a Poor Law Inspector, attributed this heavy mortality to the low physical condition of those entering:

> A large proportion of the pauper population of Kilrush Union having hitherto existed in a great measure on turnips and other vegetables, it is no wonder that debility, dysentery and diarrhoea should now prove so fatal, especially when it is considered that turnips at this season become unfit for human food.

To this one might add that the four to five years of hunger were now taking their toll. A few years previously most people had been able to make their own way to the workhouse – now a vast number were being brought on carts by their friends or relations. Dr Madden saw a large number of low-backed cars, from which the horses had been unyoked, ranged around the wall in front of the workhouse. 'On these cars the applicants for admission were lying stretched on straw, chiefly aged people of both sexes, and children, even infants. On some cars there were as many as four or five pallid, listless, emaciated, ragged children; on others, famished creatures, far gone in fever, dysentery and dropsy, unable to walk, stand or even to sit upright.'

Although many adults were now suffering very greatly, it was the children who were worst hit by disease and death, as they had even less resistance to withstand a long period of deprivation. However, the Revd Sidney Godolphin Osborne remarked that he was comforted by the fact that few starving children seemed to be in great pain:

> It has never been my lot to hear one single child, suffering from fever or dysentery, utter a moan of pain; I have seen many in the very act of

death, still not a tear, not a cry. I have scarcely ever seen one endeavour to change his or her position. I have never heard one ask for food,
for water – for anything; two, three, or four in a bed, there they lie
and die, if suffering, still ever silent, unmoved.

In Kilrush Workhouse most of the deaths were of children. Of the 213 deaths,
for example, in April 1850, 167 were of children aged 14 and under.

The children who died were undoubtedly better off than those who lived
– for in the workhouse it was simply impossible to care adequately for them.
In the Leadmore auxiliary over 1,500 'healthy' children were under the care
of two teachers. And in the Ballyera auxiliary fellow paupers were in charge
of over 120 sick children, while the same situation prevailed in another building where there were 200 children, aged two to five.

KILRUSH UNION UNDER INVESTIGATION

From the time of the publication of Captain Kennedy's reports on the evictions, Kilrush Union remained very much before the public eye, and particularly so during the financial crisis of late 1849 and early 1850. In the House of
Commons Mr Poulett Scrope made sure that his fellow MPs were kept fully
informed. On 7 March 1850 he gave a comprehensive description of what
was taking place and pointed to the inadequacy of the relief machinery. 'Who
was responsible for this refusal of relief? The Guardians threw the responsibility on the Poor Law Commissioners, and the Commissioners threw the
responsibility on the Government.' All he wanted was a commission to
inquire into the matter and suggest a remedy. But his motion was defeated, 76
to 63. Eight days later Mr Scrope was inquiring about the evictions but was
informed by Lord John Russell that there was no measure in contemplation
by Her Majesty's Government to put an end to that of which the honourable
gentleman complained.

However, official attention had been drawn to Kilrush Union, and in the
end of March Mr Bourke, a Poor Law Inspector, was sent to investigate. His
report, submitted a few weeks later, did not get to the core of the difficulty
but did make the admission that the outdoor relief being given to the people
was 'clearly inadequate to supply their wants' – as they got nothing to supply
them with lodging or clothing or any kind of food apart from the meal which
they were doled out. Meanwhile, during April, Mr Scrope continued his one-
man campaign in Parliament and eventually, in mid May, succeeded in his
objective of getting a Parliamentary Committee to inquire into Kilrush
Union. This committee had fifteen members including Sir Lucius O'Brien,
Lord Naas, Lord Arundel and Mr Scrope himself as chairman. Its terms of ref-

erence were to inquire into the administration of the Poor Law in Kilrush Union since 29 September 1848.

At the end of May the inquiry got under way and a number of witnesses including Captain Kennedy, Colonel Vandeleur, Marcus Keane and Fr Meehan, PP of Moyarta and Kilballyowen, travelled to London to give evidence. As one might expect, the evidence of people with such widely differing viewpoints did not quite tally, but, at the same time, there was no doubt in the mind of anyone about the miserable state of Kilrush Union. Two reports were drawn up, neither of which was adopted by the committee. One of these, written by Mr Scrope, concluded as follows:

> It is with regret that your committee come to the conclusion that, whether as regards the plain principles of humanity, or the literal text and admitted principle of the Poor Law of 1847, a neglect of public duty has occurred, and has occasioned a state of things disgraceful to a civilized age and country, for which some authority ought to be held responsible.

Another report, drawn up by Sir Lucius O'Brien and endorsed by many of the committee, was not as critical of the landlords as was Scrope's.

The principal people involved in relief work in West Clare were now passing from the scene. Already Captain Mann had been transferred to England, and, shortly after his return from London, Captain Kennedy learned that he had been moved to Kilkenny. This was something for which many of the Guardians had undoubtedly been agitating behind the scenes for some time, as Captain Kennedy's exposure of the numerous evictions had long since rendered him a *persona non grata*. At their meeting in mid August it was alleged that Kennedy had deliberately misinformed the public by arranging a 'showbox' at Doonbeg – thus endeavouring to blacken the character of the Guardians. This slander was let pass, but a further attack on him in October was replied to with a letter to Vandeleur in which Captain Kennedy's true feelings were revealed. In it he wrote: 'You are as prodigal of life at one time, as you are of character at another' and went on to challenge Vandeleur to a duel. Unfortunately, the newspaper report to which Captain Kennedy reacted had not been correct and the offensive statement had been made by someone other than Colonel Vandeleur. But Vandeleur did not reveal this to Kennedy, and, when the latter did discover his mistake, his apology was not accepted. Instead, Vandeleur went on to bring an action against Kennedy for his insulting letter and challenge to a duel. This case was tried at Cork Assizes in August 1851 with Kennedy's defence conducted by two very noted advocates, Isaac Butt and Sir Colman O'Loughlin. Vandeleur's action failed when the jury disagreed – seven reportedly being for acquittal and five for conviction.

Thus ended Captain Kennedy's connection with Kilrush Union, in the service of which he had worked in so dedicated a manner.

If Colonel Vandeleur and the other Guardians had disposed of one thorn in their sides when Captain Kennedy was transferred, they soon began to suffer considerable embarrassment from another direction. The Revd Sidney Godolphin Osborne, who had already shown considerable interest in Kilrush Union, began to write fairly regularly to *The Times* in the spring of 1851, giving progress reports on the destitution and misery in the area and pointing out where he considered the authorities were falling down. This interest sprang from a deep humanitarian feeling, and quite clearly there was an intense personal involvement on his part. In late March or early April he wrote:

> When, the other day, I looked on the Crystal Palace and thought of Kilrush Workhouse, as I have seen it and now know it to be, I confess I felt, as a Christian and the subject of a Christian government, utter disgust.

Osborne's letters received such attention that the Poor Law Commissioners asked Mr Lucas, their inspector at Kilrush, to submit a report, and this was published as a refutation of some points made by Osborne. Shortly afterwards two doctors, Hill and Hughes, were appointed as temporary medical inspectors to inquire into the sanitary state of Kilrush and Ennistymon Workhouses. These arrived in Kilrush in early August, but their method of procedure soon aroused grave suspicion as to the possible bias of their report. Mr Osborne claimed that they had spent a day with Colonel Vandeleur on his yacht before beginning their work, while the *Munster News* described the investigation as a farce.

In the meantime Kilrush Union was mentioned several times in the House of Commons, where Mr Scrope made an unsuccessful attempt to get lists of deaths published. Mr Osborne was also clamouring for a similar publication and eventually, on the motion of Mr Reynolds, MP, a Blue Book containing such lists was ordered to be published. It contained the names of all who died in Kilrush and Ennistymon Workhouses between 25 March 1850 and 25 March 1851 together with age, sex, cause and date of death. When a writer in the *Munster News* saw a copy of it his reaction probably summed up the feelings of many: 'No wonder it should have been so long withheld. It is an appalling and terrible compilation.' But, then, so was the whole history of Kilrush Workhouse in the previous five years.

SUPPLIES OF FOOD

In 1849 the harvest, including the crop of potatoes, was a good one, but insufficient potatoes had been sown to make any appreciable difference to the majority of the population. The stronger farmers, however, had sufficient to enable them to put a good supply on the market, and, in the first half of 1850, when the workhouse resources were under severe strain, Kilrush market was chock full of produce. On 16 February it was difficult for a pedestrian to walk along the public pathway because of the large amount of food for sale. And in May a visitor to Kilkee remarked that there was reason to believe that many had vast quantities of potatoes hoarded up for high prices in the ensuing month.

When Mr Scrope was drawing up his report for Parliament during the summer, he was impressed by the amount of food which had been available to the person with money to purchase. In this context he wrote:

> This is no case of famine; provisions have been unprecedentedly cheap and plentiful throughout the period to which the inquiries of Your Committee extend.

Whether the provisions would have proved sufficient if the money had been available is another question which cannot be answered satisfactorily. However, a very large number of people had no ready money and no prospect of obtaining any, and so they made their way to the workhouse for indoor or outdoor relief, passing the carts loaded with potatoes and other food in the streets of Kilrush. In 1851 the amount of food for sale may not have been quite so large, as the summer of 1850 saw a recurrence of blight.

Emigration

Even before the first potato failure of 1845 there was already emigration on a fairly large scale to North America from many parts of Ireland, while there was also a long-established seasonal migration to Britain from the West and north-west. Although there was certainly some emigration to America from Kilfearagh parish, it was on a very small scale. Neither was there very much migration. On this subject Captain Kennedy commented in 1850 that fewer people, in his opinion, migrated from Kilrush Union than from probably any other union in Ireland. The reason he assigned was the geographical location of the union.

In 1845 Lord Stanley commented on the Irish attitude to emigration as follows:

> The warm attachment of the Irish peasant to the locality where he was born and brought up will always make the best and most carefully conducted scheme of emigration a matter of painful sacrifice for the emigrant.

However, as potato failure, eviction and starvation crowded on top of one another in the years which followed, this attitude changed to an almost frenzied desire to sail for the New World and a new life.

The first failure of the potato crop induced quite a number of fairly well to do people to leave Ireland in the spring of 1846. After the second failure, emigration put itself forcibly before the minds of many more, both of prospective emigrants and officials. In November 1846 the Kilrush Union Guardians decided to inform the Government that an extensive system of emigration offered the only solution to the country's problems. And a few weeks later Captain Wynne, a Board of Works official in Clare, made a similar suggestion.

In the spring of 1847, when the new year's sailings resumed after the winter recess, the headlong flight from the land began. Observers at the time were of the opinion that it was the small farmer, if not the class above him, who formed the backbone of the 1847 movement. And it is at this stage, and among this group, that we get the first mention of emigration from Kilfearagh parish. In March 1847 it was stated that in Kilkee many were trying to sell their farms and lodges in order to leave the country for America.

In March 1847 Sir William Gregory, who introduced the notorious 'quarter-acre' clause, proposed another amendment to the Government's relief bill, which was accepted. According to this amendment, if the landlord of an occupier of under £5 valuation paid two-thirds of the cost of the occupier's emigration, the union might provide the remainder, even if the tenant had spent no time in the workhouse. A month later when Colonel Vandeleur, landlord and chairman of the Board of Guardians, offered free passages to America to his tenantry, he was probably trying to avail of this provision. It does not seem that very many availed of this offer, and there is no mention of any similar offer by the other landlords in Kilfearagh parish.

From the spring of 1847 on, the flow of emigration from many parts of Ireland continued to gather momentum. In West Clare, however, the movement was scarcely as pronounced as elsewhere for about two years. But as failure followed failure, with the resultant wholesale evictions of 1848 and 1849, the poor began to give very serious thought to the prospect of emigration, no matter how much they disliked it. Nevertheless, whatever their mental attitude, for most of them emigration was not a practical proposition. As Captain Kennedy wrote in early November 1848:

> The habits of the poor of this district are repugnant to emigration – they have neither the means nor energy when left unassisted.

In early 1849 Captain Studdert, RN, of Pella, Kilrush, published a pamphlet entitled *Plan for Free Emigration*, indicating the local interest in the matter. A few months later intending emigrants got a further impetus from the cholera epidemic. And in April 1849 a letter-writer to the *Freeman's Journal* from Kilrush indicated the mood of the people but also their still unresolved major problem:

> The only desire that seems to fill the minds of the people is to get out of the country to America but comparatively few among those who are most desirous to go have the means.

Meanwhile, a very partial solution to the problem of pauper emigration had come from the Government. In 1848 it was decided to select female orphans from workhouses throughout the country for emigration to Australia. The unions were to provide the girls with clothing for the journey and send them to Plymouth. And there the Emigration Commissioners took over and provided special ships to bring the girls to Australia. In December 1848 Lieutenant Henry, RN, the Emigration Commissioners' Dublin agent, visited Kilrush Workhouse and selected thirty young girls, who were later on board a ship which sailed from Plymouth in mid January 1849 with 500 orphans on board. It is quite possible that this was not the first such group to leave Kilrush, as there had been many other sailings in the previous months, and there may have been others before the general scheme came to an end in April 1850. Opposition in Australia was the reason for the cessation of this type of assisted emigration. Yet, in May 1851 we find that 150 female paupers from Ennis, Ennistymon and Kilrush Unions embarked at Dublin for

Plymouth en route to Australia. Their precise destination was probably Tasmania, because there can be little doubt that the group of forty-five from Kilrush Union which left Plymouth for there in late May or early June belonged to the same party. There is no indication that these were orphans, although this is not only possible but likely.

In 1849, as the amount of general emigration from West Clare began to increase, two ships sailed from Kilrush for Canada with 220 passengers in all. In contrast with what very often happened on these ships, they arrived in Canada with a larger number of passengers than left Ireland, as there were no deaths on board, while there was one birth. Sixteen of the passengers were assisted to emigrate by the Poor Law Union.

After the reconstitution of the Board of Guardians in autumn 1849, there could be little help for intending emigrants from the union, owing to its desperate financial situation. Nevertheless, the volume of emigration from the area increased considerably in 1850. During the late spring and early summer the local newspapers contained many paragraphs, such as the following in the *Limerick Chronicle* of 20 April:

> Cleared out this day the *Princess Victoria* for New York with 96 steerage passengers from Kilrush; the *Ariel* for Boston, 64 steerage passengers; the *Jessy* for Quebec has also cleared with 54 additional passengers from Kilrush.

And in mid May the *Clare Journal* reported:

> Emigration from this town [Kilrush] and neighbourhood is progressing on a large scale; numbers have left during the past month, and others are preparing, waiting to get remittances from their friends in America.

These American remittances, now in their infancy, were part of the key to the growing emigration from the union. One member of a family, usually the husband and father, managed to put together the fare for America. Then, when he had made a little money outside, he sent home the fare to his wife and children to enable them to join him. Thus the emphasis, and this was true throughout Ireland, was not on individual but on family emigration. In a letter to *The Times* in March 1851 Colonel Vandeleur remarked that he was happy to corroborate a fact mentioned by Mr Osborne, that large sums of money were being sent back to Ireland from America. And, probably writing in the light of his own experience at Kilrush, he went on to say that the workhouses were crowded with deserted women and children who were waiting the day when their passage money would arrive from their husbands and parents in America. Even though they might have to wait several years this money

seldom failed to arrive. In late spring 1850, just as the mass emigration movement from West Clare was eventually getting under way, Kilrush Poor Law
Guardians suggested that the rate in aid might be used for emigration purposes, but they were given what amounted to a negative response.

What had been a steady stream gathering momentum in 1850, became a
torrent in 1851. The Revd S.G. Osborne wrote in April of Kilrush Union and
elsewhere in Clare:

> Those who hope to live, hope only in the belief that they will be able
> to fly the land; those who feel they cannot fly are as men who see
> their doom.

And the *Munster News* in its first issue, six weeks later, commented:

> The emigration form this ill-fated country is terrible. All the emigra-
> tion agents in Kilrush are employed and your Port [Limerick] bears
> testimony to the extent of the business they are called upon to contract.

Nobody disputed the now widely accepted fact that the only solution to
Kilrush Union's ills was large-scale emigration. A charitable lady put a sum of
money in the hands of Osborne for emigration purposes, and he allotted
portion of this to Kilrush. The actual choice was left in the hands of Fr
Moran, CC, and Dr O'Donnell, who made the selection of families from all
the electoral districts of the union, including Kilkee. Kilrush Board of
Guardians contributed £3 to the project. On Kilrush Quay, as the emigrants
left, there were 'tears, lamentations and the wild Irish caoine,' a scene which
was to be often repeated.

About this same time the Kilrush Board of Guardians received a grant for
emigration. As soon as a rumour got around that a large number of the workhouse inmates were to be sent to America, there was an immediate rush of
applicants for admission. Meanwhile the Guardians advertised for proposals
from shipowners and others who were prepared to bring between 300 and
400 inmates of the workhouse to Quebec or some other port in British
Canada. In early August the first group of one hundred marched from the
workhouse to the quay, accompanied by the chairman and other members of
the Board, and within a few days 715 paupers had embarked at Kilrush on
four ships for Quebec. A good proportion of these, probably about half, were
from Ennistymon Union. It was also reported that 150 paupers from Kilrush
would shortly embark at Limerick for the same destination. Three months
later news came that all these Kilrush and Ennistymon emigrants had arrived
safely in Canada and had immediately secured employment. And the presence
of these in North America was an incentive to further emigration, as before
long the remittances would be arriving back in West Clare.

One wonders what were the feelings of these emigrants with their memories of evictions, starvation, and workhouse. They must have been rather similar to those expressed in a contemporary ballad to be found among the Trevelyan Papers. One verse of it perhaps sums up its general tone. It is addressed to the emigrants' former landlord:

> Now all your sooty mud wall cabins
> You may hang them on the shelf
> And when you sell out your mansion
> You can live in one yourself,
> But with the change of diet, I fear,
> Your guts they won't comply,
> When the India-buck you try it,
> Oh, your honour don't you cry.

WRECK OF THE *EDMOND*

The conditions which the people had to endure in many of the emigrant ships is well known, and the mortality rate was high – though it does appear that quite a number of the ships with people from West Clare were particularly fortunate in this regard. However, one of the greatest single tragedies associated with the exodus to America occurred when the *Edmond* was wrecked in Kilkee Bay on the night of 19-20 November 1850. Ninety-eight of her passengers and crew perished in the disaster.

The *Edmond* was a London-registered barque of 399 tons, which had been chartered by Alderman John McDonnell of Limerick to bring a party of emigrants to New York. On its way down the Shannon it called at Carrigaholt. Then, on Monday 18 November, it left Carrigaholt at 8 a.m. When it was about thirty miles out to sea a terrific gale arose and carried away all its canvas. Helpless before the storm it was blown into Kilkee Bay and stuck on the Duggerna Reef. It was soon blown off that, and, after the anchor had been lowered, it came to rest against the rocks off Sykes' House. The time was about 11.30 p.m.

Richard Russell of Limerick who was staying in Sykes' House at the time, was the first on the scene, accompanied by one of his servants. Describing what he saw, he wrote:

> At first there was no appearance of any living person on board, but as soon as we made our appearance there was one burst of horrid agony for assistance. I can never forget it – the sound will long continue fresh in my ear.

Russell sent his servant for the coastguards, two of whom soon arrived on the scene with an assistant. Meanwhile, the captain had ordered the weather rigging of the foremast to be cut, and this provided a means by which passengers were enabled to crawl from the ship to the shore. They were helped in this by the five men on the rocks. About one hundred reached safety in this manner, but, when the tide rose, it became absolutely impossible for those still remaining to get off the ship. Shortly afterwards, at about 3 a.m., it broke in two. Several people now made a vain attempt to get on to the rocks but failed and were drowned. Over fifty others were on the part of the wreck which drifted ashore on the beach at the east end, but most of them were washed overboard before safety was reached. Among those who survived this terrible journey were the members of a Crotty family who, it was said, were landed almost at their own doorstep. In all, ninety-eight people died and there were 119 survivors.

To add to the horror of the scene a number of local people, probably near death from starvation themselves, tried to get whatever plunder they could. An eyewitness wrote:

> Nothing could exceed the brutal, and, I regret to say, successful efforts of some people to plunder whatever they could lay their hands on; they actually stripped the clothes from the dead bodies, together with, of course, any money in them, which latter, it is supposed, was considerable. All the clothes, beds and property were, in the most cool and heartless manner, carried off by those unfeeling wretches, and this done in the presence of those shipwrecked creatures, who in vain had to beg even their clothes to cover their half-naked bodies.

Perhaps too harsh, a judgment, considering the circumstances of the plunderers.

Another visitor described the scene on the following day:

> I saw lying side by side, on a sail spread on the beach, many of the poor drowned ones, most of them young women and children; others were constantly being washed ashore and were laid with those already there … All that was left of her [the ship] were fragments scattered on the rocks and beach.

Thirty of the dead were heaped in the small yard before one of the lodges at the end of Marine Parade. These and the others were later buried in Kilfearagh graveyard. But for weeks later bodies were still being washed ashore.

Fr Comyn had played a prominent part in the rescue work, and, later, the Catholic priests of the parish were able to induce the people to restore much of the plundered property. Nevertheless, in early December, a number of people were fined from £5 to £20 each for concealing property taken from the wreck, while some others got gaol sentences. Even Jonas Studdert was brought to court on a similar charge, but he was acquitted on the ground that the property had been brought to his yard without his knowledge. For their rescue work Richard Russell and the coastguards were awarded the silver medal of the Royal National Institution for the Preservation of Life from Shipwreck.

Picking Up the Threads

When the potato crop failed in 1845, few suspected that the resultant hunger and distress would have appreciably different results from previous severe failures. It was obvious that a wider area was affected on this occasion, but, at the same time, it was hoped that all would be well again after the harvest of 1846. When a second failure occurred in '46 and a third followed in '47 the stage was set for a process which was, in many respects, to greatly change the way of life of the people. In Kilfearagh not only were the habits, attitudes and way of life of many people changed, but even the very appearance of the countryside was greatly altered. By 1851 it was dotted with ruined cabins, while many fields which had formerly been sown with potatoes were now again under grass .

The years 1845-51, then, undoubtedly witnessed the greatest disaster the parish had ever known and one which, in the most literal sense of the word, was almost indescribable. From an early stage writers had used very strong adjectives, such as 'terrible', 'appalling', 'horrible' etc. to describe what they had seen. These continued to be used, for want of any others, but their meaning took on a new depth and intensity as time went on.

As we saw, the condition of Kilrush Union received a good deal of publicity after the wholesale evictions had got under way. However, by the end of 1851 it had ceased to be news. The worst was now over, though the return to normality was slow. In the last full week of September 1852, for example, the workhouse had 2,683 inmates, quite a large number but significantly below the figure of 3,276 of a year previously. And in another respect this week was a very important one – it was the first since the beginning of the Famine in which no death had occurred in the workhouse. But the previous six years had seen many, very many deaths. What effect had these deaths on the population structure of the parish?

POPULATION

In the half century before 1845 the population had been rising rapidly. In 1831 it was estimated at 6,239 for Kilfearagh and 6,700 three years later. And in 1841 it was 7,137. Whatever about the precise accuracy of the 1831 figure, one thing is quite obvious – that the population was very much on the increase. All this was to change with the Famine. In 1851 the usual decennial census was held, and its figures are extremely revealing. However, in comparing them with those for 1841 a few things must be kept in mind. Firstly, when the census was taken in 1851 the state of emergency was not yet over in

West Clare, unlike other parts of the country. Secondly, there had been a significant increase in population between 1841 and 1845. Thus in the latter year the population of the parish was almost certainly over 8,000 and quite possibly much higher. Captain Mann, in a letter to Sir Randolph Routh in December 1847, mentioned that the population of Kilrush Union had increased since 1841. Captain Wynne, a Board of Works officer in Clare, was more specific:

> The Census of 1841 being pronounced universally to be no fair criterion of the present population and consequent destitution, I tested the matter in the Parish of Clondegad, Barony of Islands, where I found the present population more than a third greater than that of 1841 – this I believe to be the case in all the districts along the coast.

The figures in the accompanying table therefore only serve to give some idea of the decline between 1845 and 1851. In fact, the position was much worse. We also give the 1861 figures here to illustrate that a halt was by no means called in 1851.

KILFEARAGH PARISH

Townland	1841	1851	1861
Ballyonan	331	233	160
Baunmore	213	88	92
Corbally	587	368	237
Dough	553	405	362
Emlagh	143	119	116
Farrihy	138	86	98
Foohagh	120	98	27
Garraun	115	92	91
Kildeema	154	123	100
Kilfearagh	665	436	400
Kilkee Lower	60	31	50
Kilkee Upper	49	4	18
Kilnagalliagh	202	69	29
Knockroe	26	18	4
Leaheen	67	27	12
Lisdeen	587	354	270
Lisluinaghan	489	276	259
Moyasta	578	383	349
Termon East	239	43	44
Termon West	340	291	253
Kilkee Town	1,481	1,869	1,856
Total	7,137	5,413	4,827

It will be noted that the population of Kilkee Town had increased by almost 400 between 1841 and 1851. However, as we saw, considerable expansion took place between 1841 and 1845, so that it had probably reached 1800 by the latter date. Thus, though many of its inhabitants suffered very much during the Famine, it at least maintained its level of population – possibly being assisted by the large number of evicted country people who drifted in search of lodgings. The position of the town as a holiday resort was clearly a very great help.

If we take the rural portion of the parish alone, the results of the years 1845-1851 become very obvious:

> Rural portion 1841   5656
> Rural portion 1851   3544

The decline here is thirty-seven per cent and it was probably nearer fifty per cent between 1845 and 1851. And during the following ten years it continued, though in not quite as marked a manner.

> Rural portion 1851   3544
> Rural portion 1861   2971 (a decline of 19.2 per cent)

In some of the townlands the position was far worse than the parochial average:

	1841	1851	1868
Foohagh	120	98	27
Kilnagalliagh	202	69	29
Leaheen	67	27	12
Termon East	239	43	44

EMIGRATION

Deaths and evictions played the major part in causing the decline between 1841 and 1851. From 1851 on the continued decline was mainly caused by emigration. Almost up to this time emigration had not been an important issue in West Clare. Before the famine began, even though the population was rising and the standard of living was going down through repeated subdivision, the people's vision was bounded by the parish of their birth. They accepted the place in which they lived, for better or worse, and also the fact that they might have to go hungry at times when the harvest was not very good. However, as C.W. Hamilton pointed out, they were a very independent people who accepted the difficulties of their way of life and were prepared to face them.

The years 1846-1850 changed all this. The whole world which these people had known had collapsed about them. The food supply, always precarious, failed time and time again – underlining a fact already very evident, that there was an over-dependence on the potato. With the successive failures a vicious spiral began. The labourers and smallest farmers had to have recourse to Poor Law relief. The Poor Law rate, as a result, increased and multiplied. Farmers who were already struggling were now hit with this heavy demand, and many eventually found that they too had to join those who were depending on rather than contributing to the rate. And, of course, the landlords, in order to avoid paying the rates on small patches of ground which they had rented out, had recourse to eviction. In all this matter, too, the repeal of the corn laws did not help. Thus within a few years the whole pattern of life for several thousand people changed. Those who had formerly been independent and assured of at least the basic necessities of life found that they were reduced to a worse state than the beggars who had previously called at their doors. The beggars had always been able to get shelter for the night, but the newly evicted often found that the landlord had forbidden their neighbours to take them in. Eventually the sufferings of their wives and children forced them to swallow their pride and face towards the workhouse in Kilrush.

After eviction or a voluntary giving up of their arms, the people concerned no longer had any stake in the country. The relief afforded by the workhouse might keep them alive for the moment – but what of the future? Had they any future? It was at this stage that emigration to America came to be seen as a new hope – an opportunity of getting out of the present misery and making a fresh start in life of a kind which was impossible in Ireland. Others who still were eking out a wretched existence on their farms began to look on it in the same way. After the first emigrants had reached America they soon brought out their wives and families, and, once begun, this process went on and on. The 'Irish Emigrant's Address to his Irish Landlord', part of which has been quoted already, shows us the attitude of at least one of these to his own country:

> I'm now going to a country, where
> From Poor Rates I'll be free,
> For Poor Ireland's going to the dogs
> As fast as fast can be.

And when the immediate crisis was over a tradition of emigration had already been built up so that it continued at a frightening pace during the 1850s. No longer were the emigrants people who had to emigrate but people who wanted to emigrate. The result was that a decade later a commentator could write:

There is scarcely a family in Clare which has not some member or members in America or Australia, and remittances are constantly being sent by these exiles to their relatives at home.

PATTERN OF FARMING

With evictions and emigration the size of holdings increased. This consolidation was certainly desired by the landlords, and an opportunity to bring it about presented itself when many tenants fell heavily into arrears, particularly after the third potato failure. The wholesale evictions caused terrible suffering and were often done in a very heartless manner. However, the landlords also had their difficulties, as they found their incomes declining and their bills for poor law rates mounting. It was the waging of their own battle for self-preservation which in many cases drove them to evict and, also, on the part of those who were members of Kilrush Board of Guardians, to attempt economies which would keep down the rates. The only landlord in Kilfearagh parish whose estates actually passed into the hands of a receiver was the O'Gorman Mahon. In 1855 we find that Lisdeen was now the property of Jonas Studdert and Francis Coffey. Of the other principal landlords John MacDonnell died in June 1850 and was succeeded by his nephew, William Armstrong. Both Colonel Vandeleur and the second Marquess Conyngham survived the famine period and lived on for many years. Marcus Keane was to add a few more unhappy chapters to the story of Kilfearagh and adjoining parishes before his death in 1883.

With consolidation and a declining population there was a movement away from tillage to cattle and dairy farming. The repeal of the corn laws in 1846 also made a significant contribution to this trend. In 1862 Henry Coulter, a correspondent for *Saunders's News Letter,* could write of West Clare:

> The large farmers have converted all their arable land into grazing ground, to feed stock and make butter, instead of growing corn as they used formerly do. For instance, previously to 1846, more than 100,000 barrels of oats were annually exported from Kilrush; but the quantity now exported does not amount to 50,000 barrels a year; cattle, pigs and butter having taken the place of corn.

In 1863 Lord Conyngham obtained a patent to hold four fairs in the year in Kilkee.

Although conacre had almost disappeared during the later famine years, it again revived, and Coulter remarked on this practice in West Clare. £4 was then the general charge for an acre in the Kilkee area. The existence of conacre in the 1860s gives an indication of something which is obvious from other sources. Though the Great Famine had shaken the faith of the people in the potato, it had not broken their dependence on it. And despite the smaller population, after poor harvests there were to be many other periods of hunger though, fortunately, no famines. However, the Famine had introduced some changes. The potato crisis had induced many farmers, who had never previously done so, to sow turnips, beans and some other crops. And after 1850 they continued to do so.

EDUCATION AND RELIGION

In educational matters a significant change had come during our period with the opening of Kilkee National School in 1845. The era of the hedge schools was now drawing to a close, and, though a few may have lingered on, their days were numbered. The Irish language, too, as we saw, was very much on the decline, even before the opening of the National School. If any further impetus was needed for the movement to learn English, this was provided by the American emigration, for the purpose of which knowledge of the English language was especially useful.

The big educational question in the 1840s and 1850s was not the position of the Irish language in the National Schools but the provision of education for Irish Catholics which would be free from even the suspicion of proselytism. And this the National system provided, apart from some exceptions, mainly in the north of Ireland. The problem of proselytism was quite a live one about 1850, and in the next decade considerable efforts were made to woo and even force people away from the Catholic faith in the parishes of Moyarta and Kilballyowen. In October 1851, just as the attack in these parishes was well under way, it was reported that a sum of £75 had been sent to Kilkee for proselytising purposes, and in the following month the Revd W. Wilberforce preached in the chapels of Kilkee and Carrigaholt 'to counteract the recent fast progress of the Scriptural schools'. It does not appear, however, that any real attempt was made to concentrate on Kilfearagh parish. Perhaps the presence of the redoubtable Fr Comyn was too much of a deterrent. At any rate, when he died three years later, the *Limerick and Clare Examiner* wrote in his obituary notice:

> One circumstance highly creditable to his zeal and determination is that no souper or bible reader ever set up shop in the parish of Kilkee.

In religious matters the period 1834-51 marked the end of the penal era, which could be said to have been officially and ceremoniously closed with the Synod of Thurles in 1850. One of the purposes of this national synod was to bring the discipline of the Irish Church into line with the discipline of the universal Church and, in the process, eliminate many of the customs which had grown up during the penal times. Thus, the synod, with some insignificant exceptions, forbade the practice of performing marriages and baptisms in private houses. If Dr Cullen had his way it would also have effectively put an end to the stations by forbidding the hearing of women's confessions in private houses. In this instance the bishops who were in favour of retaining the penal customs prevailed and succeeded in obtaining a decree which still tolerated, though it did not encourage, the practice. Thus after 1850 parochial life came to be more centred on the chapels, which were also emerging from the penal style of thatched roof and bare earthen floor without any seating. It is certainly doubtful if there were any, or very many, seats in Kilkee Chapel for quite some time after it was opened.

POLITICS

In politics, as we saw, Fr Comyn was a very strong supporter of O'Connell and even though he was a close friend of Fr John Kenyon he had little sympathy with the revolutionary aspects of the Young Ireland movement. With the death of O'Connell in 1847 an era in Irish history came to a close and also a chapter in the political history of Kilfearagh parish. After the ill-fated rising of 1848 came the foundation of the Tenant Right League in 1850 and the attempts to secure an independent opposition in the decade which followed. Probably Fr Comyn's last political fight was in an election in 1853 in which the Conservative candidate for Clare, Colonel Vandeleur, was defeated. There was a general hubbub in Kilkee when the popular news came of Vandeleur's defeat. Jonas Studdert tried to intervene, and Fr Comyn attempted to restrain him. As a result Studdert brought a charge of riot and assault against Fr Comyn, while the latter, in the best Irish tradition, returned the compliment by bringing a charge of assault and riot against Studdert. The affair ended when Studdert withdrew his charges. It does show, however, that there was still plenty of political vigour in the parish and that it only awaited a good cause and effective leadership to be brought once more to the pitch of enthusiasm which had been aroused for O'Connell and his policies. Indeed, the more one studies local politics in the middle of the nineteenth century, the more aware one becomes of the intense involvement of the people. Politics for them meant not just an occasional election but provided a good deal of the brightness in their lives as they travelled to meetings, signed petitions and lit the omnipresent tar barrels on the occasion of the visit of a patriot such as Smith O'Brien to Kilkee.

RECREATION

If politics can be regarded as one facet of the people's diversion, then there was no major change here around 1851 apart from the different issues and policies involved. The Kilkee Races also survived the changing times, though some of the other amusements associated with them, such as shawl-dancing, seem to have died out. The faction fighters, too, are heard of no more after the Famine, though this is fairly true of the country as a whole in the 1850s, in which there were only a few instances of the old time faction fights. However if faction fights were doomed to die a natural death in any event, this was not true of hurling, which appears to have been quite popular in the early 1840s and is never mentioned again after the Famine. One can only conclude that the general run of life was so dislocated that men had no longer the opportunity, desire or energy to hurl for several years – and by the time the situation had changed again the old tradition had been broken. It was Gaelic football alone which was played in the area after the foundation of the GAA in the 1880s.

HOLIDAY RESORT

In the 1830s and early 1840s Kilkee was a booming holiday resort and was undoubtedly one of the most popular and fashionable in Ireland. New lodges were constantly being built, new businesses were opening every year and the general impression was of a go-ahead, rapidly expanding town. Then, during the famine years, although large crowds of visitors still continued to frequent the resort, business was not, as one would expect, quite as good as in the preceding decade. However, the coming of the Famine also meant an end to the rapid expansion which had been taking place, and, once lost, this impetus was never recovered again. Very few new lodges were built during these years, and there was a slight recession rather than a further expansion in trade. When normality returned in the early 1850s, it probably did not occur to anybody at first that things were any different from a decade earlier. However, the era of expansion was now over, and, although further building did take place over the next few decades, it was no longer at the same pace as before the Famine and could in general be regarded as consolidation. A decline had not set in, but development had been very largely arrested. The town was still a very popular and fashionable resort. In August 1853, for example, we find two grandsons of Louis Philippe of France among the visitors, along with many other members of the French nobility. And two years later the *Limerick Chronicle* informs us:

> On Monday a large assemblage of the rank, beauty and fashion of the neighbourhood attended in Merton Square to take part in the new and popular game of croquet and to enjoy the delightful strains of a band, hired for the occasion.

This shows that Kilkee was still very much to the fore with the latest fashions, as croquet was as yet very much a novelty in Britain and Ireland.

That Kilkee did not continue to develop as previously during the 1850s and thereafter may be in part due to the expansion of railways about this time, thereby making access easier to very many places at home and abroad which could hitherto be reached only after journeys involving extreme discomfort. Between Limerick and Kilkee the only advance was a railway between the former and Foynes, from which place the boat could be taken to Kilrush. From 1845 on, there were repeated unsuccessful attempts to secure a railway between Kilrush and Kilkee. Whereas in 1835 Kilkee was one of the most easily accessible resorts in the country, the position had radically changed twenty years later through developments elsewhere and the lack of them in West Clare.

To conclude. From 1834 to 1851 was not a very long period in time. But a new world had emerged for the people of Kilfearagh parish by the latter date. Many things had changed because of the Great Famine; others had changed for different reasons which also came to the fore about this time. And if the people's world had changed, so also had many of their attitudes to the environment in which they found themselves. But they were still a deeply religious people, still deeply interested in politics and still prepared to down tools to urge on the horses of their choice at the Kilkee Races.

Notes

The text to which these notes relate is identified by the *page number*; the bold word(s) indicate the place on the page to which the note that follows relates. The references link up with the author or short title or Parliamentary Paper reference number – all of which are listed in full in the **Bibliography** – or an abbreviation in the following list:

3321-79	National Library of Ireland MSS 3321-79, which contain newspaper clippings relating to County Clare
CJ	Clare Journal
Devon Commission	Evidence taken before her Majesty's commissioners of inquiry into the state of the law and practice in respect to the occupation of land in Ireland – Parliamentary Papers 1845 XX (evidence taken at Kilrush).
DUM	Dublin University Magazine
LC	Limerick Chronicle
L and CE	Limerick and Clare Examiner
LEP and CS	Limerick Evening Post and Clare Sentinel
LR	Limerick Reporter
LR and TV	Limerick Reporter and Tipperary Vindicator
NLI	National Library of Ireland
NMAJ	North Munster Antiquarian Journal
PP	Parliamentary Papers
RCP	Relief Commission Papers

Page 11 **Limerick Chronicle:** 24 May 1845. **most abundant:** 27 Aug. 1845. **13 September:** quoted in Woodham-Smith, 40. **calamity:** *CJ*, 16 Oct. 1845.

Page 12 **Mr Fleming:** *LR*, 7 Nov. 1845. **masses:** *LC*, 8 Nov. 1845. **government commission:** Edwards and Williams, 210-1. **statement:** Woodham-Smith, 48-9. **progress of the disease:** Edwards and Williams, 213.

Page 13 **Studdert:** *RCP 1845-7, Inspecting Officers, Reports*, 80, Studdert to Relief Commissioners, 9 Dec. 1845. **Morris:** ibid., 141, Morriss to Relief Commissioners, 12 December 1845. **Hancock:** ibid., 173½ (*sic*), Hancock to Relief Commissioners, 13 Dec. 1845. **Corca Baiscinn:** O'Donovan, *Annals*, a.799 (recte 804). **very little fish:** *RCP 1845-7, Inspecting Officers, Reports*, 136; *LR*, 16 Dec. 1846. **immediate employment:** *LR*, 12 Dec. 1845. **these statistics:** *The Times*, 5 Dec. 1845 (3325, 97).

Page 14 **Railway Bills:** *LR*, 2 Dec. 1845. **Moyasta evictions:** *CJ*, 19 Jan. 1846. **Peel's plan:** Woodham-Smith, 61-2. **new roads:** With regard to the second proposal, Colonel Harry Jones, Chairman of the Board of Works, was rather pessimistic. In the places worst hit by distress the more important roads had been laid down in previous famines and there was little left to be done except roads leading to farms. **Board of Works representative:** Woodham-Smith, 63-4. **first such meeting:** *PP* 1846 XXXVII (41), 9-13, Routh to Trevelyan, 15 Jan. 1846.

Page 15 **Kilkee meeting:** cf. *CJ*, 15 Jan. 1846; *Tipperary Vindicator*, 14 Jan. 1846.

local committee: The committee included four honorary members – Mr Burton, C.W. Hamilton, John Westropp of Limerick and Captain Creagh. There were thirteen in the working committee including Fr Comyn, Fr W. O'Brien, CC, the Revd J. Martin, Dr Tuite, Dr Griffin and Robert Fitzgerald. **rival memorial:** _LC_, 14 Jan. 1846 (3326, 5). **Studdert:** _RCP 1845-7, Inspecting Officers, Reports,_ 343, Jonas Studdert to Sir Lucius O'Brien, 11 Jan. 1846.

Page 16 **Hamilton:** ibid., 343, Hamilton to Sir Lucius O'Brien, 12 Jan. 1846. **18 January:** _LR,_ 27 Jan. 1846. **16 March:** _Trevelyan Papers,_ Mann to Trevelyan, 16 March 1847, T64/362A(10).

Page 17 **local contributions:** _PP_ 1846 XXXVII(41), 10, Routh to Trevelyan, 15 Jan. 1846. **Studdert:** _RCP 1845-7, Inspecting Officers, Reports,_ 343, Jonas Studdert to Sir Lucius O'Brien, 11 Jan. 1846. **Hamilton:** _PP_ 1846 XXXVII(41), 10, Routh to Trevelyan, 15 Jan. 1846. **local relief committee:** This was undoubtedly different to that set up on 10 January, although a number of people would be common to both. **in the final analysis:** _LR,_ 6 March 1846.

Page 18 **disease expected:** _PP_ 1846 XXXVII(479), 3. **22 February:** _RCP 1845-7, Inspecting Officers, Reports,_ 504. **Kildimo memorial; tickets for corn:** _PP_ 1846 XXXVII(429), 8, 3, 7. **portion ... nearly full:** _PP_ 1846 XXXVII(41), 224. **Routh:** ibid., 82, Routh to Trevelyan, 28 March 1846. **31 March:** ibid., 86, Routh to Trevelyan, 31 March 1846. **in early May:** _RCP 1845-7, Inspecting Officers, Reports,_ 2113, Mann to Sir James Dombrain, 6 May 1846. **Conyngham:** The _L and CE_ of 20 May 1846 reported that one landlord with an annual rental of £1,200 gave £10. There is no such contribution mentioned in the Revd James Martin's letter. Perhaps it arrived after 12 May – from Lord Conyngham.

Page 19 **12 May:** _RCP 1845-7 (Clare),_ Revd J. Martin to Relief Commissioners, 12 May 1846. **£23:** _PP_ 1846 XXXVII(41), 224. **strolling beggars:** _LC,_ 16 May 1846 (3326, 44). **Messrs Wallace, Sharpe:** _LC,_ 1 April 1846 (326, 28). **efforts of Comyn and Hogan:** _Tipperary Vindicator,_ 29 Jan. 1846; _RCP 1845-7, Inspecting Officers, Reports,_ 392; _LR,_ 23 Jan., 31 Mar. 1846; _CJ,_ 26 Jan. 1846.

Page 20 **bad fishing:** _LR,_ 20 March 1846. **favourable hearing:** _CJ,_ 9 Feb. 1846. **Dowling's reply:** _LR,_ 20 March 1846. **9 March:** _LC,_ 28 March 1846 (3326, 27-8). **£5000:** Woodham-Smith, 79. **Peel:** _LC,_ 28 March 1846 (3326, 28). **release from pawn:** _LC,_ 21 March 1846 (3326, 25). **loan-office:** _CJ,_ 27 April 1846. **gratitude:** _LR,_ 12 May 1846.

Page 21 **Mann:** _Trevelyan Papers,_ Mann to Trevelyan, 15 Nov. 1847, T64/367A(3). **hill-cutting:** _RCP 1845-7, Inspecting Officers, Reports,_ 573, Russell to Board of Works, 18 Feb. 1846. **Kilfearagh projects:** _PP_ 1846 XXXVII(41), 273-4. **employment tickets:** _LC,_ 18 Feb. 1846 (3326, 11); Edwards and Williams, 219.

Page 22 **10d.:** _LR,_ 6 March 1846. **7 March:** _PP_ 1846 XXXVII (429), 3. **250:** _L and CE,_ 11 March 1846. **embankment of cliff:** _LC,_ 25 March, 11 April 1846 (3326, 27, 33); _L and CE,_ 20 May 1846. **coast road:** _L and CE,_ 20 May 1846. This coast road was, in fact, never constructed. **Conyngham:** _LC,_ 25 March 1846 (3326, 27). **£100:** _CJ,_ 27 April 1846. **10,870:** _PP_ 1846 XXXVII(41), 82, 86, 87. **620:** _L and CE,_ 20 May 1846. **rates of payment:** _RCP 1846-7, Accounts etc. relative to Relief Districts 1846,_ Circular answered by Kilrush Relief Committee. **independence of character:** _RCP 1845-7, Inspecting Officers, Reports,_ 431, C.W. Hamilton to Relief Commission, 30 Jan. 1846.

Page 23 **reject it:** ibid., 3084, Revd James Martin to Relief Commissioners, 9 June 1846. **Trevelyan:** Woodham-Smith, 76.

Page 24 **central depot:** _L and CE,_ 13 May 1846; _Trevelyan Papers,_ Mann to Trevelyan, 15 Nov. 1847, T64/367A(3). **minor depots:** _RCP 1845-7 (Clare),_ Letter of

Revd James Martin to unnamed recipient, 8 Oct. 1846; *Inspecting Officers, Reports*, 2113, Mann to Sir James Dombrain, 6 May 1846. **stirrabout:** *Trevelyan Papers*, Mann to Trevelyan, 15 Nov. 1847, T64/367A(3). **three days:** *L and CE*, 13 May 1846. **expert knowledge:** *Trevelyan Papers*, Mann to Routh, 14 Dec. 1847, T64/369B(1). **querns:** *PP* 1847 LI, 239, Mann to Trevelyan, 5 Nov. 1846; O'Rourke, *Great Irish Famine*, 242. The handmills produced in Kilkee may have been used for other purposes than grinding corn. It was stated before the committee inquiring into illicit distillation in 1854 that handmills were used in making spirits illicitly – *PP* 1854 X, 66. **Shetlands:** *PP* 1847 LI, 211, Trevelyan to Routh, 30 Oct. 1846.

Page 25 **querns:** ibid., 274, Mann to Trevelyan, 16 Nov. 1846. **Mann to Routh:** *Trevelyan Papers*, 14 Dec. 1847, T64/3693B(1). The prices must have gone down from the 10s. to 12s. previously mentioned by Mann as few of the cabin-holders would have such sums at their disposal. **Twisleton:** *Trevelyan Papers*, 3 Jan. 1848, T64/367C(1). **slow torture:** Woodham Smith, 76. **early March:** *PP* 1847 LI, 152, Mann to Crafer, 11 Oct. 1846 (describing the situation in early March). *Clare Journal:* 30 April 1846.

Page 26 **memorial:** *LR*, 6 Jan. 1846; *Tipperary Vindicator*, 14 Jan. 1846. **bluestone:** *LC*, 14 March 1846 (3326, 16). **chairman:** *RCP 1845-7, Inspecting Officers, Reports*, 650, Mr G.H. Fitzgerald to Mr E. Lucas, 28 Feb. 1846. **last line:** *RCP 1845-7, Constables' Reports on Potato Crops 1846*.

Page 27 **para. 1:** *RCP 1845-7, Inspecting Officers, Reports*, 4662 (enclosed with 4796), Kilkee Relief Commission to General Relief Committee for Ireland, n.d. (July 1846); 4965, Jonas Studdert to Wm. Stanley, n.d. **Lisdeen and Farrihy:** *Trevelyan Papers*, T64/366C(1); and Mann to Trevelyan, 5 Nov. 1847, T64/367A(3). **what was left:** *LR*, 11 Sep. 1846. **11 August:** *PP* 1847 LI, 6, Mr White to Assistant Commissary General Wood, 11 Aug. 1846.

Page 28 **previous year:** *Tipperary Vindicator*, 12 Aug. 1846. **Mann:** Trevelyan Papers, Mann to Trevelyan, 15 Nov. 1847, T64/367A(3); cf. Woodham-Smith, 106-8.

Page 29 **27 August:** *RCP 1845-7, Inspecting Officers, Reports*, 5581, Fr Malachy Duggan to Relief Commissioners, 27 Aug 1846. **23 August:** *LR*, 28 Aug. 1846; *CJ*, 31 Aug. 1846. **sympathetic hearing:** *L and CE*, 16 Sept. 1846; *LR*, 11 Sep. 1846.

Page 30 **new roads:** *LR*, 25 Sep. 1846. **Bentinck bill:** Woodham-Smith, 180-1. **4 September:** *LR*, 25 Sep. 1846. **'orgy':** Woodham-Smith, 113. **£10,077:** *Trevelyan Papers*, T64/362B. **storm at sea:** *LR*, 25, 29 Sep. 1846; *LC*, 30 Sep. 1846 (3326, 87).

Page 31 **prices:** A few days previously the *Clare Journal* of 8 October had stated that Indian meal was 2s. 9d. a stone in Kilrush. **he went on:** *PP* 1847 LI, 151/2, Mann to Mr Graver, 11 Oct. 1846. **para. 2:** *Tipperary Vindicator*, 9 Oct. 1847; *LC*, 21 Oct. 1846 (3326, 97); *L and CE*, 24 Oct. 1846; *CJ*, 26 Oct. 1846. **Martin:** *Relief Commission Papers 1845-7 (Clare)*, Letter of Revd J. Martin, 8 Oct. 1846. **reply:** *PP* 1847 LI, 175.

Page 32 **prices lowered:** *Trevelyan Papers*, Mann to Trevelyan, 15 Nov. 1847, T64/367A(3). **decided to issue meal:** *PP* 1847 LI, 298. **750:** *LC*, 4 Nov. 1846 (3326, 105). **one in three:** *The Tablet*, 21 Nov. 1846. Clare's nearest rivals were Roscommon (20, 106), Limerick (18,282), Galway (14,714), Mayo (13,149) and Cork (10,566). By contrast, in Dublin only 48 were employed. **8d.:** *Tipperary Vindicator*, 11 Nov. 1846. **Friends:** Society of Friends, *Transactions of the Central Relief Committee of the Society of Friends during the Famine in Ireland in 1846 and 1847*, Dublin, 1852, 179-180. On 13 Nov. 1846 the Central Relief Committee of the Society of Friends was set up in Dublin. It was to do very fine work during the Famine, and as its first object it decided to obtain 'trustworthy information respecting the real state of the more remote districts'. Hence the visit to West Clare.

Page 33 **Mann:** *Trevelyan Papers*, Mann to Trevelyan, 15 Nov. 1847, T64/367A(3).
Griffin: *Relief Commission Papers 1845-7 (Clare)*, Dr John Griffin to Sir R. Routh, 8
March 1847. **Wynne:** *PP* 1847 L, 270-1, Captain Wynne to Board of Works, 19 Nov.
1846. **Hutchinson:** ibid., 281. **a month later:** ibid., 483. **reduce rents:** Woodham-
Smith, 123. **Keane:** *LC*, 11 Nov. 1846 (3326, 111). **notice at Doonbeg:** *PP* 1847 LI,
240.

Page 34 **Kilrush memorial:** *CJ*, 26 Nov. 1846. **Wynne:** *Trevelyan Papers*, Capt.
Wynne to Capt. Larcom, 5 Dec. 1846, T64/362B; and *PP* 1847 L, 436, Capt Wynne
to Lieut Col Jones, 24 Dec. 1846.

Page 35 **colonial lands:** *CJ*, 7 Jan. 1847; *LC*, 2 Jan. 1847 (3327, 1). **an assurance:**
CJ, 7 Jan. 1847; *LC*, 6 Jan. 1847 (3327, 2). **Central:** This was the General Central
Relief Committee, set up a short time previously on 29 Dec. 1846, under the presi-
dency of Lord Kildare, eldest son of the Duke of Leinster. The name used in Fr
Comyn's letter to the Duke might tend to suggest the Central Relief Committee of
the Society of Friends, but we know that Fr Comyn afterwards received a donation
from the General Central Relief Committee.

Page 36 **para. 1:** *LR*, 12 Jan. 1847; *LC*, 20 Jan. 1847 (3327, 10).

Page 37 **soup kitchen:** *PP* 1847 LII (333), 53, Capt Mann to Commissary-General
Hewetson, 22 Jan. 1847; *LC*, 27 Jan. 1847 (3327), 13); *LR*, 26 Feb. 1847. In early 1847
the Catholics of Liverpool sent Dr Kennedy £142 17s. per the Archbishop of Cashel,
for the relief of the destitute poor of Killaloe diocese. During February many parishes,
like Kilfearagh, acknowledged the receipt of £5 from Dr Kennedy – probably the
division of the £142. *Chronicle: LC*, 27 Jan. 1847 (3327, 13). **early April:** *L and CE*,
17 April 1847. **Friends' gifts:** see *LC*, 10 April 1847 (3327, 41); 1 May 1847 (3327,
48); 5 June 1847 (3327, 56); 4 Aug. 1847 (3327, 93). *Reporter: LR*, 26 Feb. 1847.

Page 38 **fear of disease:** *CJ*, 4 March 1847. **onset of fever:** *The Tablet*, 14 Aug.
1847 (letter to Fr Meehan); *CJ*, 15 March 1847; Woodham Smith, 202-3, *The Tablet*,
14 Aug. 1847; *LC*, 23 June 1847 (3327, 59). **priest's work:** *The Tablet*, 14 Aug. 1847.
emigration: *LC*, 24 March 1847 (3327, 35). **Mann:** *Trevelyan Papers,* Captain Mann
to Trevelyan, 16 March 1847, T64/362A(10).

Page 39 **conacre:** *The Tablet*, 23 Jan. 1847.

Page 40 **Mann:** *Trevelyan Papers*, Mann to Trevelyan, 15 Nov. 1847, T64/367A(3);
Woodham-Smith, 286. **acreage under turnips:** *Trevelyan Papers*, T64/366B.
Twisleton: ibid., T64/368B. **little turf:** *LR*, 4 June 1847. **murder case:** *LC*, 23
June 1847 (3327, 59); *CJ*, 26 July 1847; *Tipperary Vindicator*, 19 June 1847. *Reporter:*
LR, 27 July 1847.

Page 41 **mid-August:** *L and CE*, 21 Aug. 1847. **prematurely:** *L and CE*, 20
Nov. 1847. **closing dates:** Woodham-Smith, 302-3, 307. **memorials:** *LC*, 29 Sep.
1847 (3327, 114); *LR*, 15 Oct. and 2 Nov., 1847.

Page 42 **Mann:** *Trevelyan Papers*, Captain Mann to Trevelyan, 15 Nov. 1847,
T64/367A(3). **Looker-On:** *LC*, 6 Nov. 1847 (3327, 126).

Page 43 **para. 1:** Woodham-Smith, 307-8; Edwards and Williams, 251. **entering**
the workhouse: ibid., 253. The Gregory clause was later relaxed in May 1848.
Twisleton: *Trevelyan Papers,* Twisleton to Trevelyan, 13 Jan. 1848, T64/367C(1).
Trevelyan even asked: Woodham-Smith, 316. **Inspector:** These inspectors examined the accounts and administration of the union to which they were assigned and
reported incompetence and maladministration to the Poor Law Commissioners. They
also kept the Commissioners informed of affairs in the district.

Page 44 **a week later:** *PP* 1847-8 LIV (29), 155, Capt Kennedy to Poor Law
Comms., 11 Nov. 1847. See also ibid. 157, Capt Kennedy to Poor Law Comms., 18
Nov. 1847. **1849:** *Trevelyan Papers*, T64/370C(1), Printed memo marked confidential.

obituary: *LR and TV*, 28 March 1851. **drowning:** *LC*, 23 Oct. 1847 (3327, 122). **lack of stamina:** *The Tablet*, 14 Aug. 1847.

Page 45 **no buyers:** *PP* 1847-8 LVI, 790, Kennedy to Poor Law Comms., 11 Feb. 1848. **40 men:** *PP* 1847-8 XXXVII (213), 284. **slower than others:** *PP* 1847-8 LVI, 790, Kennedy to Poor Law Comms., 11 Feb. 1848. **flax:** *L and CE*, 27 Nov. 1847; *CJ*, 29 Nov. 1847. **stray potatoes:** *LC*, 13 Nov. 1847 (3327, 127). **Kennedy:** *PP* 1847-8 LV, 381, Kennedy to Poor Law Comms., 25 Nov. 1847.

Page 46 **winter of death:** *L and CE*, 6 and 20 Nov. 1847. **para. 4:** *PP* 1847-8 LIV (29), 155, Kennedy to Poor Law Comms., 11 Nov. 1847; *PP* 1847-8 LV, 394, Kennedy to Poor Law Comms., 30 Dec. 1847; ibid., 402, Kennedy to Poor Law Comms., 19 Jan. 1848; ibid., 394, Kennedy to Poor Law Comms., 30 Dec. 1847; *RCP 1845-7, Poor Law Commissioners, Reports and Returns, 1844-7*, Kennedy to Poor Law Comms., 18 Nov. 1847; *PP* 1847-8 LIV (29), 155, Kennedy to Poor Law Comms., 11 Nov. 1847. **not to provide coffins:** *The Tablet*, 4 Dec. 1847. **Madden:** T.M. Madden (ed.), *Memoirs*, 244.

Page 47 **Madden:** ibid., 252-3. **no shroud:** *LR and TV*, 2 May 1851. **Nation:** quoted in *Munster News*, 9 August 1851.

Page 48 **lodgings:** *LC*, 28 Aug. 1850. **6000:** *PP* 1847-8 LIV (29), 157, Kennedy to Poor Law Commissioners, 18 Nov. 1847. **Doonbeg:** *LC*, 18 Dec. 1847 (3327), 136). **Mann:** *Trevelyan Papers*, Mann to Routh, 14 Dec. 1847, T64/369B(1); and ibid., Mann to unnamed recipient (possibly Routh), 22 Dec. 1847, T64/366C(2). **stealing:** *LC*, 5 Jan. 1848 (3328, 1). **robbed:** *LC*, 1 March 1848 (3328, 35). **broken into:** *LC*, 15 March 1848 (3328, 30). **traders:** *LC*, 22 Jan. 1848 (3328, 22). **Kennedy:** *PP* 1847-8 LVI, 801, Capt Kennedy to Poor Law Commissioners, 1 March 1848.

Page 49 **Mann:** *Trevelyan Papers*, Mann to unnamed recipient (probably Trevelyan), 11 Feb. 1848, T64/370C(4). **gifts:** *LC*, 26 Jan. 1848 (3328, 23); 12 Feb. 1848 (3328, 31); 22 April 1848 (3328, 64); 26 Feb. 1848 (3328, 34); 22 April 1848 (3328, 64); 2 Sep. 1848 (3328, 106). **13 February:** *Trevelyan Papers*, Mann to unnamed recipient, 13 Feb. 1848, T64/370C(4).

Page 50 **making clothes:** ibid., Mann to Trevelyan, 12 Jan. 1848, T64/367C(1); *L and CE*, 25 April 1848; *Trevelyan Papers*, Mann to (probably) Trevelyan, 11 Feb. 1842, T64/370c(4); *L and CE*, 15 April 1848. **half a million:** *Trevelyan Papers*, T64/367B(1). **Mann:** ibid., Mann to (probably) Trevelyan, 11 Feb. 1848, T64/3706(4). **not to be charged:** *National School Register* (Clare, vol. 1). **Russell promise:** Woodham-Smith, 367. **came to an end:** 13 Sep. 1848 (3328, 108).

Page 51 **para. 1:** Nowlan, *The Politics of Repeal*, 206-7. **21 June:** *LR*, 27 June 1848. **weeks later:** *Tipperary Vindicator*, 22 July 1848. **Lord Clare Club:** *LC*, 22 July and 23 Aug. 1848 (3328, 95 and 103). **O'Gorman escape:** *LC*, 19 Aug. 1848 (3328, 102) and see I. Murphy, *The Diocese of Killaloe, 1800-1850*, Dublin, 1992, pp 205-7; *LR*, 18 Aug. 1848; *CJ*, 24 Aug. 1848. **final para.:** *L and CE*, 17 June 1848; *LC*, 22 July 1848 (3328, 95); *L and CE*, 2 Aug. and 12 Aug. 1848.

Page 53 **Mann:** *Trevelyan Papers*, Mann to (probably) Routh, 22 Dec. 1847, T64/366C(2); 20 Nov. 1847, T64/367A(3). **Reporter:** *LR*, 24 Nov. 1848. **Kennedy:** *PP* 1849 XLIX (315), 4-5, Capt Kennedy to Poor Law Commissioners, 6 April 1848. Not all landlords acted in such a manner. The *Clare Journal* of 22 June 1848 reported the sale of his yacht by Mr Burton of Carrigaholt to make money for the poor. **petition:** *Tipperary Vindicator*, 29 Dec. 1847. **Mann:** *Trevelyan Papers*, Mann to Routh, 14 Dec. 1847, T64/369B(1); Mann to Trevelyan, 21 Dec. 1847, T64/369B(1). **nothing further:** Fr Hartney, CC, Kilfearagh, was present at a Tenant Right demonstration in Ennis in late Oct. 1850 (*LR and TV*, 1 Nov. 1850).

Page 54 **demolished:** *PP* 1849 XLIX (315) 30 (Report of Vice-Guardians of

Kilrush Union, 21 Oct. 1848). **Osborne:** Godolphin Osborne, *Gleanings*, 26–8. **'kene':** Osborne mistakenly uses the word 'skene'. Perhaps it is a misprint.

Page 55 **Hogan incident:** *L and CE*, 2 Dec. 1848. **destruction went on:** PP 1849 XLIX (315), 7, Capt Kennedy to Commissioners, 5 July 1848. *Reporter: L and CE*, 11 March 1848.

Page 56 **para. 1:** *PP* 1849 XLIX (315), 30, 31, 33, 35, 37; *The Tablet*, 9 Dec. 1848; *PP* 1849 XLIX (315), 36. **put out to die:** *PP* 1849 XLIX (315), 7, Capt Kennedy to Commissioners, 5 July 1848.

Page 57 **to his host:** W.F. Butler, *Autobiography*, 12. **benefactor:** *L and CE*, 9 Dec. 1848. **Foley:** ibid., 12 Feb. 1848. **Blue Book:** In *PP* 1849 XLIX – *Reports and Returns relating to Evictions in the Kilrush Union.* **some effect:** *The Tablet*, 9 June 1849.

Page 58 **Keane:** *CJ*, 20 Aug. 1849. **Scrope:** *CJ*, 4 Oct. 1849. *Gleanings:* Osborne, 21. **reporter:** *Illustrated London News*, 22 Dec. 1849. **Jarvey:** *L and CS*, 12 Sep. 1849.

Page 60 **Kennedy:** *PP* 1847-8 LIV(29), 156, Kennedy to Poor Law Comms., 18 Nov. 1847; *PP* 1847-8 LV, 388, Kennedy to Poor Law Comms., 16 Dec. 1847. **final para.:** ibid., 381, Kennedy to Poor Law Comms., 25 Nov. 1847; *RCP 1845-7, Poor Law Commissioners, Reports and Returns 1844-7*, Kennedy to Poor Law Comms., 11 Nov. 1847; *PP* 1847-8 LV, 385, Kennedy to Poor Law Comms., 2 Dec. 1847; ibid., 381, Kennedy to Poor Law Comms., 25 Nov. 1847; ibid., 391, Poor Law Comms. to Kennedy, 27 Dec. 1847.

Page 61 **appalling sight** and **mid November:** *PP* 1847-8 LIV(29), 155-6, Kennedy to Comms., 11 and 18 Nov. **cash as well:** *RCP 1845-7, Poor Law Commissioners, Reports and Returns 1844-7*, W. Stanley, Sec. Poor Law Commission, to Capt Kennedy, 16 Nov. 1847; Kennedy to Poor Law Comms., 18 Nov. 1847. **Scrope:** *PP* 1850 XI (529), x. **Mann:** *Trevelyan Papers*, Mann to Routh, 14 Dec. 1847, T64/369B(1).

Page 62 **three hundred:** *PP* 1847-8 LV, 386, Kennedy to Poor Law Comms., 2 Dec. 1847. **Kennedy report:** *RCP 1845-7, Poor Law Commissioners, Reports and Returns 1844-7*, Kennedy to Poor Law Comms., 2 Dec. 1847. This section of his report was not printed with the remainder of it in the Parliamentary Papers. **31 December:** *PP* 1847-8 LV, 388, Poor Law Comms. to Kennedy, 21 Dec. 1847.

Page 63 **centre page:** ibid., 395, Kennedy to Poor Law Comms., 1 Jan. 1848; *PP* 1847-8 LIV(313), 239; *PP* 1847-8 LV, 398, Kennedy to Poor Law Comms., 13 Jan. 1848. **Mann:** Trevelyan Papers, Mann to (probably) Trevelyan, 11 Feb. 1848, T64/370C(4). **bacon store:** ibid. **60:** *Trevelyan Papers*, Mann to Trevelyan, 12 Jan. 1848, T64/367C(1). **nurses scared:** *PP* 1847-8 LV, 394, Kennedy to Poor Law Comms., 30 Dec. 1847.

Page 64 **Slaughter House:** *Trevelyan Papers*, Mann to (probably) Trevelyan, 11 Feb. 1848, T64/370C(4). **Hamilton:** *RCP 1845-7, Inspecting Officers, Reports*, 421, C.W. Hamilton to Relief Commission, 30 Jan. 1846. **Madden:** T.M. Madden (ed.), *Memoirs*, 244. **final para.:** *PP* 1847-8 LVI, 791, Kennedy to Poor Law Comms., 18 Feb. 1848; **Trevelyan Papers**, Report of Captain Kennedy, 24 Feb. 1848, T64/369B(3); *L and CE*, 23 Feb. 1848.

Page 65 **utterly incompetent:** *PP* 1847-8 LVI, 793, Kennedy to Poor Law Comms., 18 Feb. 1848. **no credit:** *Trevelyan Papers*, Report of Capt Kennedy, 24 Feb. 1848, T64/369B(3). **distress warrants:** ibid., Mann to Trevelyan, 27 Feb. 1848, T64/370C(4). **a great abuse:** ibid., Trevelyan to Twisleton, 2 March 1848, T64/370C(4). **order dissolving:** *PP* 1847-8, LVI, 800. **financial:** *Trevelyan Papers*, Twisleton to Trevelyan, 6 Feb. 1848, T64/370c(4). **4s. 11d.:** Although the average rate in Kilrush Union was 4s. 11d., it was 6s. 10d. in Kilkee electoral division. **29 January:** *Trevelyan Papers*, Abstract of Papers relating to the buying and collection of Poor Rates in certain unions, T64/370C(3). **inevitable:** On 3 February 1848 Twisleton informed Trevelyan that his main object in appointing paid Guardians was to prevent the Irish Unions making demands on the national funds at a time when, if carried on to any great extent, this might be 'seriously injurious to the Empire'. In his view it was essential to throw Ireland on its own resources as far as possible. The best means for extracting money from unwilling ratepayers was through paid Guardians – T64/370C(4).

Page 66 **a larger rate:** *Trevelyan Papers*, Twisleton to Trevelyan, 15 Aug. 1848, T64/367B(2). **current rate:** *LC*, 22 April 1848 (3328, 64). **shoulders:** *LC*, 10 May 1848 (3328, 71); 9 Sep. 1848 (3328, 108); 13 Sep. 1848 (3328, 108). **special report:** *Trevelyan Papers*, Mann to Trevelyan, 12 Jan. 1848, T64/367C(1). **Phelan:** *LC*, 23 Feb. 1848 (3328, 33). **'unbounded confidence':** ibid.; *LC*, 11 March 1848 (3328, 36). **8,032:** *Trevelyan Papers*, T64/366B. **Times:** 25 Aug. 1848 (3328, 103). **Twisleton:** *Trevelyan Papers*, Twisleton to Trevelyan, 15 Aug. 1848, T64/367B(2).

Page 67 **'empire will reel':** *LC*, 18 Oct. 1848 (3328, 115). **Kennedy's reports:** *PP* 1849 XLVIII(87), 53, Kennedy to Poor Law Comms., 12 Nov. 1848. **outbreak of cholera:** *CJ*, 2 April 1849; Woodham-Smith, 380-1. **'choleraphobia':** *PP* 1849 XLVIII(171), 29, Kennedy to Poor Law Comms., 3 April 1849. **O'Donnell:** *CJ*, 9 April 1849. **Griffin:** *LR*, 1 May 1849.

Page 68 **summer season:** *LR*, 31 July 1849; *LC*, 25 Aug. 1849 (3329, 73). **visitors' reports:** *L and CE*, 15 Aug. and 8 Sep. 1849. **drownings:** *LC*, 15 Sep. 1849 (3329, 77). **'too weak to row':** *PP* 1850 XI(529), 108 (evidence of Fr Meehan of Carrigaholt). **Monsell:** later Lord Emly. **favourably impressed:** *LR*, 12, 16 Oct. 1849; *L and CE*, 13 Oct. 1849. In these newspaper reports Stephen de Vere is mentioned three times and Aubrey de Vere is mentioned once. However, it is clear from his *Recollections* that Aubrey was accompanying Arundel and Monsell. And he makes no mention of his brother, Stephen. **Aubrey de Vere:** *Recollections*, 250.

Page 69 **Journal:** *CJ*, 12, 19 Nov. 1849. **Treasury advances:** Woodham-Smith, 379. **£4,500:** *L and CE*, 10 Nov. 1849. **5½d.:** *LC*, 14 Nov. 1849 (3329, 142-3). **£7,000:** *L and CE*, 1 Dec. 1849; *LC*, 21 Nov. 1849 (3329, 143). **not the rates but the rents:** *L and CE*, 24 Nov. 1849.

Page 70 **ensuing week:** *L and CE*, 24 Nov. 1849. **places distant:** During their period of office the Vice-Guardians appointed medical officers to each of the electoral divisions of the union (Dr Griffin in Kilkee district). These treated the sick poor in their own houses and were allowed to order rice, milk, oatmeal or other such food for them. With the abandonment of this service such sick people would now have to enter the workhouse (*PP* 1850 XI(529), 133). **13,000:** *L and CE*, 1 Dec. 1849. **reporter:** ibid., 8 Dec. 1849. **five days:** *PP* 1850 XI(529), xi. **sent home:** *L and CE*, 8 Dec. 1849. **memorial:** *PP* 1850 XI(529), 16.

Page 71 **drowning:** *CJ*, 17 Dec. 1849; *LR*, 18 Dec. 1849. **poem:** *Munster News*, 25 Sep. 1867. **Reporter:** *LR*, 18 Dec. 1849.

Page 72 **shellfish:** *PP* 1850 XI(529), 28, 30, 107. **hordes of poor:** ibid., 27 (Capt Kennedy to Poor Law Commissioners, 27 Dec. 1849). **reporters:** *L and CE*, 5 and 9 Jan. 1850. **lifeline:** *CJ*, 7 Jan. 1850 **reporters excluded:** *The Tablet*, 5 Jan. 1850.

Page 73 **lost all dependence:** Printed Memorandum marked Confidential. Vandeleur to Mr Stanley (for Poor Law Commissioners), 31 Dec. 1849, T64/370C(1). **get rid of Kennedy:** *L and CE*, 12 Jan. 1850. **cut off again:** *L and CE*, 2 Feb. 1850. **supplementary:** *The Tablet*, 2 Feb. 1850. **extreme necessity:** ibid., 9 Feb. 1850. **exporting work:** *L and CE*, 16 Jan., 6 Feb. 1850. **end of March:** *CJ*, 1 April 1850. **Times:** Quoted in *CJ*, 8 April 1850. **pay less rates:** *CJ*, 25 April 1850. **entire year:** *LC*, 24 July 1850. **Examiner:** *L and CE*, 28 Nov. 1849.

Page 74 **5000:** *PP* 1850 XI(529), 240. **250:** *L and CE*, 9 Feb. 1850. **2 February:** *PP*

1850 XI(529), 57. **unwarrantable:** *PP* 1851 XLIX(279), 64, Kennedy to Poor Law Commissioners, 13 May 1850. **diet:** ibid., 47.

Page 75 **late February:** *The Tablet*, 2 March 1850. **8d.:** T.M. Madden (ed.), *Memoirs*, 247-8. **milk:** The milk in the children's diet in early 1850 was later changed to artificial milk because a good deal of difficulty was experienced in getting milk supplies. In May 1850 the milk contractor admitted that she skimmed the milk before delivery (*LC*, 22 May 1850). **two beds:** *PP* 1851 XLIX(209), 51. **three patients:** *CJ*, 24 April 1851. **final para.:** *L and CE*, 23 Feb. 1850. **Kennedy:** *PP* 1850 XI(529), 50.

Page 76 **Vandeleur:** ibid., 131. **decrease:** Madden, op. cit., 247; *PP* 1850 XI(529), 3, evidence of Captain Kennedy. **140:** *PP* 1851 XLIX (279), 2-26. **Lucas:** *PP* 1851 XLIX (271), 4. **unfit for human food:** This was written in mid April. **Madden:** *Memoirs*, 244. **Osborne:** *Gleanings*, 18.

Page 77 **167:** *PP* 1851 XLIX (279), 2-6. **200:** *PP* 1850 XI (529), 80-1. **76 to 63:** *The Tablet*, 9 March 1850. **Russell:** ibid., 23 March 1850. **Bourke:** *L and CE*, 3 April 1850; 1 May 1850. **April:** see *The Tablet*, 27 April 1850.

Page 78 **28 Sept:** *PP* 1850 XI (529), ii. The evidence was published in this volume of Parliamentary Papers. **Scrope:** ibid., xii-xiii. **O'Brien:** *CJ*, 28 Oct. 1850. **Mann transfer:** Woodham-Smith, 367. **Kennedy moved:** *L and CE*, 31 July 1850. **'showbox':** *CJ*, 22 Aug. 1850. **Kennedy letter:** *L and CE*, 9 Nov. 1850. Captain Kennedy had already at this stage been dismissed from his Kilkenny post by the Poor Law Commissioners although the local Guardians unanimously petitioned for his retention. **apology not accepted:** *The Tablet*, 25 January, 1851. **action failed:** *L and CE*, 13 Aug. 1851.

Page 79 **so dedicated:** In that same year Kennedy was appointed Governor of Gambia and in 1852 was transferred to Sierra Leone. From 1854 to 1862 he was Governor of Western Australia and held several other appointments in the colonial service during the next fifteen years. In 1877 he returned to Australia as Governor of Queensland. This was his last post as he died en route to England from there in 1883. He was knighted in 1868. **Osborne:** e.g. *CJ*, 17 March 1851 (Vandeleur to *The Times* rebutting Osborne); *CJ*, 7 April 1851. **Crystal Palace:** *LR and TV*, 8 April 1851. **Lucas:** *PP* 1851 XLIX (271). **temp. inspectors:** *LC*, 25 June 1851; *The Tablet*, 9 August 1851; *LC*, 16 Aug. 1851; *Munster News*, 6 Sep. 1851. **lists of deaths:** *LR and TV*, 8 April 1851; *CJ*, 17 April 1851; *LC*, 9 April 1851; *PP* 1851 XLIX (279); *Munster News*, 3 March 1852 and 8 Nov. 1851. **1849:** *PP* 1850 XI (529), 9 (evidence of Captain Kennedy).

Page 80 **16 February:** *CJ*, 18 Feb. 1850. **visitor:** *LC*, 11 May, 1850 (3330, 32). **Scrope:** *PP* 1850 XI (529), xii. **recurrence:** *LR and TV*, 6 Aug. 1850.

Page 81 **already emigration:** Fr Comyn's brother, Thomas, emigrated to the USA in 1822. Some of the letters he wrote home still survive in *Comyn Correspondence*. **Kennedy:** *PP* 1850 XI(529), 68. **1845:** quoted in Woodham-Smith, 206. **spring of 1846:** ibid., 214. **November:** *The Times*, 28 Nov. 1846 (3326, 114). **Wynne:** *Trevelyan Papers*, Wynne to Captain Larcom, 5 Dec. 1846, T64/362B. **backbone:** Edwards and Williams, 321. **March 1847:** *LC*, 24 March 1847 (3327, 35). **Gregory clause:** see Oliver MacDonagh, 'The Poor Law', 32.

Page 82 **Vandeleur:** *LC*, 21 April 1847 (3327, 45). **Kennedy:** *PP* 1849 XLVIII(87), 51, Capt Kennedy to Commissioners, 7 Nov. 1848. **Studdert:** *LC*, 10 Feb. 1849 (3329, 14). **April 1849:** quoted In *Tipperary Vindicator*, 28 April 1849. **girls to Australia:** Robins, 'Irish Orphan Emigration' 357-7. **30 girls:** *CJ*, 21 Dec. 1848. **500:** *L and CE*, 17 Jan. 1849. **Opposition:** Robins, op. cit., 387. **150:** *LR and TV*, 16 May 1851.

Page 83 **early June:** *L and CE*, 4 June 1851. **two ships:** *PP* 1850 XL, 14-17.
Journal: 13 May 1850. **family emigration:** Edwards and Williams, 328.

Page 84 **seldom failed:** *CJ*, 17 March 1851. **negative response:** *CJ*, 20 May
1850. **Osborne:** *The Tablet*, 26 April 1851. *News:* 7 June 1851. **actual choice, etc.:**
ibid., 18 June, 25 June. **final para.:** *CJ*, 19 June 1851; *LC*, 25 June 1851; *CJ*, 7 Aug.
1851; *The Tablet*, 16 Aug. 1851; *LC*, 9 Aug. 1851; *CJ*, 24 Nov. 1851.

Page 85 **Trevelyan:** Enclosed in *Trevelyan Papers*, T64/370c(1). **Edmond disaster:**
LC 23 and 27 Nov. 1850.

Page 86 **ditto:** *LR* and *TV*, 22 Nov. 1850; *The Tablet*, 30 Nov. 1850. **Another
visitor:** W.R. Le Fanu, *Seventy Years of Irish Life*, 92-3. **four weeks later:** *LC*, 23
Nov. 1850; *L and CE*, 14 Dec. 1850.

Page 87 **rewards and punishments:** *LC*, 11 Dec. 1850; *CJ*, 5 Dec. 1850; *The
Tablet*, 18 Jan. 1851.

Page 88 **first week with no death:** *Munster News*, 29 Sep. 1851. **statistics:** *PP*
1835 XXXIII, 228c.

Page 89 **Mann:** *Trevelyan Papers*, Mann to Routh, 14 Dec. 1847, T64/369B(1).
Wynne: ibid., Wynne to Capt. Larcom, 5 Dec. 1846, T64/362B. **statistics:** Census
of 1871 (Munster).

Page 90 **37 per cent:** Between 1841 and 1851 the population decline was 15.5 per
cent in Leinster, 16 per cent in Ulster, 23.5 per cent in Munster and 28.6 per cent in
Connacht (Woodham-Smith, 412). It is clear from these figures that West Clare was
among the worst hit areas in the country and the devastation in its rural parts was
scarcely equalled elsewhere. **Foohagh:** Property of John MacDonnell and later of his
nephew, William Armstrong. **Kilnagalliagh:** Property of Samuel Cox and Anthony
Hickman (*Griffith's Valuation, Co. Clare*, Dublin 1855). **Leaheen and Tarmon East:**
Hickman property. **Hamilton:** *RCP 1845-7, Inspecting Officers, Reports*, 421, C.W.
Hamilton to Relief Commission, 30 Jan. 1846.

Page 91 **Address:** *Trevelyan Papers*, T64/3700(1). **commentator:** Henry Coulter,
The West of Ireland, 56.

Page 92 **Lisdeen:** *Griffith's Valuation, Co. Clare*. **MacDonnell:** Burke, *Landed
Gentry*, ii, 1176. **survived:** ibid., ii, 1882, 276. **Coulter:** Coulter, *The West of Ireland*,
59. **1863:** *Munster News*, 10 June 1863. **£4:** Coulter, op. cit., 71.

Page 93 **1850:** ibid., 65. **1851:** *Munster News*, 22 October 1851; *LC*, 29 Nov. 1851.
Examiner: 8 Nov. 1854.

Page 94 **a decree:** cf. Barry 'The Legislation ...', 138-45. **Kenyon:** John Kenyon
preached a panegyric at Fr Comyn's month's mind. **affair ended:** *LC*, 6, 23 July
1853.

Page 95 **French nobility:** *LC*, 27 Aug. 1853. **Chronicle:** 19 Sep. 1855.

Bibliography

MANUSCRIPTS

Dublin: National Library of Ireland:
Dunboy Collection of Newspaper clippings relating to Co. Clare (3321-3379).
Dublin: Public Record Office
Relief Commission Papers (Clare) 1845-7.
R.C.P., Constables' Reports, Potato Crops 1846.
R.C.P., 1845-7, Returns of Correspondence etc., Commissariat Office 1846-7.
R.C.P. 1845-7, Poor Law Commissioners, Reports and Returns 1844-7.
R.C.P. 1845-7, Inspecting Officers, Reports.
R.C.P. 1846-7, Accounts etc. relative to Relief Districts 1846.
National Schools Register, County Series, Co. Clare, vol. 1.
London: Public Record Office
Trevelyan Papers (T64).
Ennis: Killaloe Diocesan Archives
Canon Clancy Papers
Comyn Correspondence

PARLIAMENTARY PAPERS

First Report of the Commissioners of Public Instruction, Ireland, with Appendix, PP 1835 XXXIII.
Reports from Commissioners, Poor Inquiry (Ireland), PP 1835 XXXII (i), and (ii).
Evidence taken before Her Majesty's commissioners of inquiry into the state of the law and practice in respect to the occupation of land in Ireland: together with appendix and plans, PP 1845 XIX-XXI.
Correspondence explanatory of the Measures adopted by Her Majesty's Government for the Relief of Distress arising from the failure of the Potato Crop in Ireland, PP 1846 XXXVII(41)
Weekly Reports of the Scarcity Commission, showing the progress of disease in the potatoes, the complaints which have been made, and the applications for relief in the course of the month of March 1846, PP 1846 XXXVII(429).
Abstracts of the most serious representations made by the several medical superintendents of Public Institutions (Dispensaries etc.), PP 1846 XXXVII(479).
Correspondence from July 1846 to January 1847, relative to the measures adopted for the relief of distress in Ireland, with maps, plans etc. (Board of Works Series), PP 1847 L.
Correspondence from July 1846 to January 1847, relating to the measures adopted for the Relief of Distress (Commissariat series), PP 1847 LI.
Correspondence from January to March 1847, relative to the measures adopted for the Relief of Distress in Ireland (Board of Works), Second Part, PP 1847 LII.
Correspondence from January to March 1847, relating to the measures adopted for the Relief of Distress in Ireland (Commissariat series), Second Part, PP 1847 LII(333).
Correspondence from July 1846 to January 1847, relating to measures adopted for the Relief of the Distress in Ireland and Scotland (Fisheries series), PP 1847 LIII(379).

First Annual Report of Commissioners of Irish Poor Laws, PP 1847-8 XXXIII(387).

Sixteenth Report of the Commissioners of Public Works and Appendix, PP 1847-8 XXXVII(213).

Papers relating to Proceeding for the Relief of Distress and State of the Unions and Workhouses in Ireland:
> *Fourth series 1848*, PP 1847-8 LIV(29)
> *Fifth series 1848*, PP 1847-8 LV.
> *Sixth series 1848*, PP 1847-8 LVI.
> *Seventh series 1848*, PP 1847-8 LVI(313).
> *Eighth series*, PP 1849 XLVIII(221).

Further Papers relating to the Aid afforded to the Distressed Unions in the West of Ireland, PP 1849 XLVIII (17), (87), (171).

Reports and Returns relating to Evictions in the Kilrush Union, PP 1849 XLIX (315)

Report from Select Committee on Kilrush Union, together with proceedings of committee, minutes of evidence etc., PP 1850 XI(529).

Copy of Despatch, dated 11 February 1850, transmitting Report from the Chief Emigration Agent at Canada for the year 1849 and Documents showing the facilities afforded to Emigrants from Europe for reaching the interior by the completion of the St Lawrence Canals, PP 1850 XL.

Copies of Correspondence between the Poor Law Commissioners and their Inspectors relative to the statements contained in an extract from a book entitled 'Gleanings in the West of Ireland', PP 1851 XLVIII(209).

Copy of a Report made to the Poor Law Commissioners by Mr Lucas, Temporary Inspector in charge of Kilrush Union, in reference to certain statements regarding the management of Kilrush Union, contained in a letter signed 'S. Godolphin Osborne', which appeared in the 'Times' newspaper of the 31st day of March 1851, PP 1851 XLVIII(271).

Return of the Deaths in the Kilrush and Ennistymon Workhouses, Hospitals etc. from 25 March 1850 until 25 March 1851, with the Name, Age, Sex, Cause and Date of Death, Date of Admission, with the Observation of the Medical Officer on each case; copy of the Dietary in the Kilrush and Ennistymon Workhouses during the above period etc., PP 1851 XLVIII(279).

Report from the Select Committee of the House of Lords appointed to consider the consequences of extending the functions of the Constabulary in ireland to the suppression or prevention of illicit distillation; and to report thereon to the house; together with the minutes of evidence, PP 1854 X.

BOOKS AND ARTICLES

An ex-MP (Henry Lambert), *A Memoir of Ireland In 1850*, Dublin, 1851.

Barry, P.C., SJ, 'The Legislation of the Synod of Thurles, 1850' in *Irish Theological Quarterly*, XXVI,2 (April 1959), 131-46.

Beckett, J.C., *The Making of Modern Ireland 1603-1923*, London, 1966.

British Association, *British Association for the Relief of extreme distress in Ireland and Scotland: Report with correspondence of the agents, tables etc., and a list of subscribers*, London, 1849.

Burke, Sir Bernard, *A Genealogical and Heraldic Dictionary of the Peerage and Baronetage together with Memoirs of the Privy Councillors and Knights*, 40th ed., London, 1878.

——, *A Genealogical and Heraldic History of the Landed Gentry of Great Britain and Ireland*, 2 vols., London: i, 8th ed., 1894; ii, 7th ed., 1886.

Butler, Lieut. General Sir W.F., *Sir William Butler, An Autoboigraphy*, London, 1911.

Census of Ireland 1871, Province of Munster, Dublin, 1874.

Connell, K.H. *The Population of Ireland, 1750-1845*, Oxford, 1950.

——, *Irish Peasant Society, Four Historical Essays*, Oxford, 1968.

Coulter, Henry, *The West of Ireland: its Existing Condition and Prospects*, Dublin, 1862.

Cullen, L.M., *Life in Ireland*, London and New York, 1968.

de Vere, Aubrey, *Recollections of Aubrey de Vere*, New York and London, 1897.

Dictionary of National Biography, Oxford, 1937-8.

Edwards, R.D. and Williams, T.D. (eds.), *The Great Famine, Studies in Irish History 1854-52*, Dublin, 1956.

Evans, E. Estyn, *Irish Heritage*, Dundalk, 1967.

Foster, Thomas Campbell, *Letters on the Condition of the People of Ireland*, London, 1846.

Freeman, T.W., *Pre-Famine Ireland*, Manchester, 1957.

Fraser, James, *Handbook for Travellers in Ireland descriptive of its Scenery, Towns, Seats, Antiquities etc.*, 4th ed., Dublin, 1854.

Frost, James, *The History and Topography of the County of Clare*, Dublin, 1893.

Griffith's Valuation, Co. Clare, Dublin, 1855.

Indian Relief Fund Trustees, *Distress in Ireland. Report of the Trustees of the Indian Relief Fund showing the distribution of the sum of £13,919. 14s. 2d. commencing the 24th April and ending the 31st December 1846*, Dublin, 1847.

Irish Catholic Directory (Registry), Dublin, 1836.

Knox, Alexander, *The Irish Watering Places, their Climate, Scenery and Accommodation*, Dublin, 1845.

Lampson, G. Locker, *A Consideration of the State of Ireland in the 19th Century*, London, 1907.

Le Fanu, W.R., *Seventy Years of Irish Life*, London, 1893.

Mac Cumhghaill, Brian, *Sean de hOra*, Baile Atha Cliath, 1856.

MacDonagh, Oliver, 'The Poor Law, Emigration and the Irish Question, 1830-55' in *Christus Rex* xii,1 (Jan. 1958), 26-37.

McDowell, R.B. (ed.), *Social Life in Ireland 1800-45*, Dublin, 1957.

——, *The Irish Administration 1801-1914*, London and Toronto, 1964.

MacIntyre, Angus, *The Liberator, Danel O'Conell and the Irish Party 1830-1847*, London, 1965.

McNeill, D.B., *Coastal Passenger Steamers and Inland Navigations in the South of Ireland*, Belfast Transport Museum, 1965.

Madden, T.M. (ed.), *The Memoirs (Chiefly Autobiographical) from 1798 to 1886 of Richard Robert Madden, M.P., F.R.C.S.*, London, 1891.

Malone, Sylvester, *Tenant Wrong Illustrated in a Nutshell, or a History of Kilkee in relation to Landlordism during the past seven years in a letter addressed to the Rt Hon W.E. Gladstone, MP*, Dublin, 1867.

Maxwell, Constantia, *The Stranger in Ireland*, London, 1954.

Nowlan, Kevin B., *The Politics of Repeal. A Study in the Relations between Great Britain and Ireland, 1841-1850*, London and Toronto, 1965.

O'Brien, R. Barry, *Fifty Years of Concessions to Ireland 1831-1881*, 2 vols., London, n.d.

O'Brien, W.P., *The Great Famine in Ireland and a Retrospect of the Fifty Years 1845-1895*, London, 1896.

O'Donovan, John (ed.), *Annals of the Kingdom of Ireland by the Four Masters*, 7 vols., Dublin, 1851.

O'Fiaich, Tomás, 'Sources for Irish Social History, 1750-1850', in *Christus Rex* xii.1 (Jan. 1958), 3-14.

O'Neill, Thomas P., 'The Irish Workhouses during the Great Famine' in *Christus Rex* xii.1 (Jan. 1958), 15-25.

O'Rourke, John, *The History of the Great Irish Famine of 1847 with notices of earlier Irish famines*, Dublin, n.d.

Osborne, S. Godolphin, *Gleanings in the West of Ireland*, London, 1850.

Parliamentary Gazetteer of Ireland, 10 parts, Dublin, London and Edinburgh, 1845-6.

Report of the Commissioners appointed to take the Census of Ireland for the year 1841, Dublin, 1843.

Robins, Joseph A., 'Irish Orphan Emigration to Australia 1848-1850' in *Studies* (Winter 1968), 372-387.

Society of Friends, *Transactions of the Central Relief Committee of the Society of Friends during the Famine in Ireland in 1846 and 1847*, Dublin 1852.

Woodham-Smith, Cecil, *The Great Hunger. Ireland, 1845-9*, London, 1962.

Index